Few realities are more ~~p...~~ one make rebellious dec ~~...~~
As a pastor and counselo ~~...~~ ~~...~~ with countless parents,
spouses, siblings, and friends agonizing with them over how to
love someone who refuses to take help. *Letting Go* is a book I wish
could go back and give to each one of those hurting people. It is a
book I will give to every one of them in the future. This book by
Dave Harvey and Paul Gilbert is essential reading for all those
with wayward loved ones and for all of us who are called to walk
with them in the pain.

> DR. HEATH LAMBERT, Executive Director, Association
> of Certified Biblical Counselors; author, *A Theology
> of Biblical Counseling* and *Finally Free*

One of the most difficult decisions any Christian spouse or parent has to make is when to say, "Enough! Our love isn't helping
you. It's time that you felt the weight of your choices." Guilt,
shame, anger, responsibility, and blame get mixed together in
a confusing and poisonous brew . . . parents disagree, friends
offer unasked for opinions, and all the time you're struggling to
answer the one question that's above all else: What is the most
loving thing I can do for my beloved prodigal? In their extraor-
dinarily helpful book, pastors and counselors Dave Harvey and
Paul Gilbert offer practical help for parents, spouses, and friends
who have found themselves in the unenviable position of loving
someone who has completely gone off the rails. They will walk
with you as you consider your options and help you process your
decisions. But most importantly, they will point you to Christ.
I'm really thankful for this book . . . and you will be too.

> ELYSE FITZPATRICK, coauthor, *Give them Grace*

If you've suffered the unreturned love of a prodigal child or spouse, this book is for you. I commend Dave and Paul for writing so insightfully and sympathetically—with biblical conviction—on this complex and controversial topic. Their counsel should be wisely heeded, so that we might learn to love our prodigals in a way that directs them toward the Father's open arms.

> COLLIN HANSEN, editorial director of the Gospel
> Coalition; author, *Blind Spots: Becoming a Courageous,*
> *Compassionate, and Commissioned Church*

All hell breaking loose at home is not an "if" but a "when." You will be crying out for counsel and comfort, and *Letting Go* is crisis theology at its best. Harvey and Gilbert bring clarity to the confusion, Spirit-driven comfort to the chaos, and wisdom for loving your prodigal spouse, sibling, friend, or child.

> DANIEL MONTGOMERY, Lead Pastor of Sojourn
> Community Church, Louisville

Do you know the excruciating pain of loving a prodigal? You are in good company—so does God. Billons of us. It is the story arc of the Bible. How should you love your prodigal? Read this book. Harvey's and Gilbert's wise biblical counsel is rich in compassion, sympathy, and perhaps best of all, empathy. They will point you to hope.

> JON BLOOM, cofounder and Chair of Desiring God;
> author, *Not By Sight* and *Don't Follow Your Heart*

Jesus calls us as born-again children of God to love our enemies. As difficult as that is, in some cases loving a prodigal is even harder. Someone who was close now is distant. Intimacy disintegrates into apathy or perhaps even hostility. The prodigal shows no interest in reconciliation. The burden becomes heavier and heavier, slowly grinding down your heart and your faith. Endurance weakens into exhaustion. Prayers go unanswered. Hope fades. Is this you? If so, maybe it's time to let the prodigal go. In this book, seasoned pastors Dave Harvey and Paul Gilbert will help you with the decisions involved in whether, when, and how to let go.

DON WHITNEY, Professor of Biblical Spiritual and Associate Dean, The Southern Baptist Theological Seminary; author, *Spiritual Disciplines for the Christian Life*

It's always an honor to be asked to endorse a new book by authors I respect, but this time it's a privilege. I need *Letting Go*—I need the wisdom and gospel rhythms my brothers have poured into all 192 pages of their timely tome. Sometimes loving well involves showing "wayward souls" the door, entrusting them to the God who raises the dead. Dave and Paul, thanks for reminding me that none of us is called to be the fourth member of the Trinity.

SCOTTY SMITH, Teacher in Residence—West End Community Church, Nashville

When we are faced with letting go of a wayward spouse or child, we need the wisest of companions to comfort, guide, and even challenge us. Dave and Paul are those companions. They give no trite formulas or one-size-fits-all. Instead, they remind us of God's intimate familiarity with our troubles and how he says more than we might think. Expect them to lead you into humble confidence and resilient hope.

ED WELCH, Ph.D., faculty and counselor, CCEF

This compassionate and wise book gives voice to the disorienting shame, bitterness, weariness, and fear when foraging for love amid the brutal relational conditions of a prodigal world. Like a kind and sturdy friend who's walked in our shoes, it gives us room to vent, grace to be understood, counsel to get through the next hour, the next day. Most of all, rugged love recovers us to the healing sanity and unshakeable provision of Jesus. A superb help for our work of pastoral care. A sage companion for our human wrestling with love.

ZACK ESWINE, author, *Spurgeon's Sorrows: Realistic Hope for those Who Suffer from Depression*; pastor, Riverside Church, Webster Groves, Missouri

Trying to love weak and rebellious people who don't want to change is a confusing, exhausting, and painful undertaking. Quite often wise love looks different than we could imagine and flies against our deepest fears and idolatries. This book brings two vital things together, wisdom and love. Both are crucial and both are elusive. This book will help parents, pastors, spouses, and friends to walk patiently and purposefully alongside other weak sinners in need of change and mercy. The fuel for this journey is no other than God's relentless pursuit and endless patience with all of his prodigal children. The authors faithfully point us to the perfect rugged love and sweet patience of our Savior, Jesus Christ, as the model for all our efforts to forgive as we have been forgiven.

BARBARA DUGUID, author, *Extravagant Grace* and *Prone to Wander*

With biblical wisdom and pastoral gentleness, Dave Harvey and Paul Gilbert have crafted an excellent help for those facing the unique challenge of giving grace to those who spurn it. I am grateful for this important book. *Letting Go* does wonderful justice to the complexity and the versatility of true Christian love.

JARED C. WILSON, Director of Content Strategy, Midwestern Baptist Theological Seminary; author, *Gospel Wakefulness* and *Unparalleled*

LETTING GO

Other Resources From Dave Harvey

Books

When Sinners Say "I Do": Discovering The Power Of The Gospel For Marriage (Shepherd Press)

When Sinners Say "I Do" Study Guide (Shepherd Press)

Am I Called? The Summons To Pastoral Ministry (Crossway Publishing)

Rescuing Ambition (Crossway Publishing)

Video Series

When Sinners Say "I Do" DVD Series (Shepherd Press)

Other

Am I Called (www.AmICalled.com) is a leadership resource from Dave Harvey and friends, dedicated to helping men understand ministry (church planting, eldership, pastoral, ministry leadership). On the website you'll find a ministry assessment test, interviews with well-known leaders, articles for leaders and those aspiring to leadership, and a host of other resources.

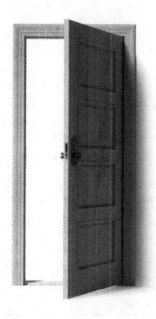

LETTING GO

Rugged Love for Wayward Souls

DAVE HARVEY AND PAUL GILBERT

ZONDERVAN

Letting Go
Copyright © 2016 by David T. Harvey and Paul Byron Gilbert

This title is also available as a Zondervan ebook.

Requests for information should be addressed to:
Zondervan, *3900 Sparks Dr. SE, Grand Rapids, Michigan 49546*

Library of Congress Cataloging-in-Publication Data

Names: Harvey, David T. (David Thomas), 1960- author. | Gilbert, Paul,
  1969- author.
Title: Letting go : rugged love for wayward souls / Dave Harvey and Paul Gilbert.
Description: Grand Rapids, MI : Zondervan, [2016] | Includes bibliographical
  references.
Identifiers: LCCN 2016009655 | ISBN 9780310523536 (softcover)
Subjects: LCSH: Love—Religious aspects—Christianity. | Interpersonal
  conflict—Religious aspects—Christianity. | Forgiveness—Religious aspects—
  Christianity. | Prodigal son (Parable) | Rejection (Psychology)—Religious
  aspects—Christianity.
Classification: LCC BV4639 .H243 2016 | DDC 241/.4—dc23 LC record available at
  https://lccn.loc.gov/2016009655

Art direction: Tammy Johnson
Interior design: Denise Froehlich

Printed in the United States of America

HB 09.13.2017

Dave:
To my beautiful daughters, Alyce and
Shelby ("Pumpkin" & "Lovey"),
Who sojourned restlessly in a broken world,
Until they found the irresistible draw of the Deeper Magic,
Which tames the soul, heals the wounds,
And gives Love a name above all others.

Paul:
To all of those at Four Oaks Church who have wrestled with
and waited in hope for the wayward in their lives. It has
been the greatest pleasure and privilege to serve you these
twenty years—I am looking forward with you to that Day
when Jesus returns and "all the prodigals run home."

Contents

Contents

Foreword

I have a problem. There are things I say that I firmly believe, but at a street level I don't live like I *truly* believe them. For example, the Bible paints for us a cover-to-cover portrait of a world that is disastrously broken, a world that does not function the way God intended. Yet the Bible says something else about this brokenness, something that is even harder for us to accept. It tells us that the ravages of the fall not only exist outside of us— they exist *inside* of us. The disaster of the fall in Eden is not just environmental, it is deeply personal. Particularly for the readers of this book.

Between the "already" of our conversion and the "not yet" of our home-going, God has called us to follow him in this broken world. This means that every hardship we face is not an interruption or a failure of God's grand plan, it is an integral part of it. We should not be shocked, angry, or discouraged when we face the difficulties this book addresses, as if something out of the ordinary is happening to us. These hardships do not mean that the world is out of God's control. Yes, it is out of *our* control, but the Bible tells us that God knows. He is there. He understands the situation in which he has placed us.

The Bible reveals God as a tender and understanding Redeemer who welcomes you to cry out to him. He won't turn his back on your angst and confusion. He won't tell you to quit crying when someone you love goes rogue. He knows what you're facing and he cares. He knows what his plan has exposed you to, and he knows that it will make you cry. He says to you, "Come to me and I will hear your cries, and I will answer them."

Accepting what the Bible says about the world we live in opens the door to two very important experiences with God:

1. *Accepting what the Bible says about the brokenness of this world enables you to admit the full depth of your need.* There is a delusion out there that there are two classes of people, the capable and the needy. I can't count the number of people who have come to me for counsel who were embarrassed and ashamed that they had problems and needed my help. Why did they feel this shame? They felt it because they were believing something that is not true. They had bought the lie that there is a class of independently capable people who have the ability to deal with whatever life brings their way. The Bible is clear that these people do not exist. We're *all* broken, and we *all* live in a tragically broken world. None of us have the ability to control what needs to be controlled, to fix what needs to be fixed, or to do what needs to be done.

So I am not surprised that marriages break up and friends betray one another. I'm not surprised that domestic violence exists and that people who have been taught the truth end up forsaking it or that people destroy the lives of others by their selfishness. In truth, I'm amazed that this doesn't happen more often. I'm amazed at how God patiently and faithfully exercises his restraining grace. I'm amazed by how many marriages do make it, how many parents truly want what is best for their children, and how many people really do desire to do what is right.

The Bible forces us to admit that we have no ability whatsoever to change the people around us in the ways that matter most. We have little ability to control the people, situations, and locations around us, and at the level of our heart's desire, we are more like than unlike the selfish and rebellious ones who have hurt us so. This leads us to the second truth that opens the door to experience God's grace in the midst of our pain and hurt.

2. *This humble, biblical neediness is the doorway to real biblical hope.* I have written this before, but I will repeat it here: hopelessness is the only doorway to real and lasting hope. Your Bible doesn't just present you with a dark and broken world. In fact, brokenness is not even the Bible's central theme. The Bible tells us that at the center of all that exists is a God of glorious love, incalculable wisdom, unshakable sovereignty, almighty power, and amazing grace, who willingly unleashes his glory for our good. Grace is the central story of the Bible—the love of God defeating the evil of human sin. The Bible's main theme is not sadness, it is the comfort of God. The biblical story doesn't end in grief, but in unfettered joy. But the first steps on that pathway to joy require admitting your need, confessing your inability, and owning your grief. There is no shame in being hurt and hopeless. The hopeless and needy are the ones who are welcomed into the tender, understanding arms of a God of eternal love.

This is why I am so thankful for the book you are about to read. I am thankful because it has stimulated me to think about these truths again, as I'm sure it will for you as well. It will yank you back to reality and call you to face hardship with honesty and humility. It will welcome you to the freedom of not trying to do what you cannot do. It will call you out of your shame. It will help you to know that in your grief you are not alone. It will put tender words of understanding to your groans. It will invite you out of the hiding into the light.

I loved this book. It is very much needed, and so very helpful. I say this because too many of us refuse to "let go," and we spend our lives fighting battles we will not win. Others have already "let go" and yet they still don't know what to do with their grief and shame. For them, this tool could not be more timely.

I pray *Letting Go* finds you in your place of need, and when it does, that you let it take you by the hand and lead you from where you are to that better place where, by God's grace, He has called you to be.

Paul David Tripp
April 28, 2016

Acknowledgments

If you've ever visited a hall of fame, you know it's typically a society's attempt to acknowledge extraordinary contributions from those who performed at the highest levels. Permit us, if you will, to stretch the analogy because we have our own *Letting Go* hall of fame. It's not a location but a conviction, a deeply rooted, abiding awareness that this project would not have come about without the amazing performances of these MVPs—most-valuable-people.

Walk the hall with us for a minute, so you can see that we are ordinary men surrounded by extraordinary people.

DAVE

To Kimm, Tyler, Janelle, Alyce, Rich, Asa, Shelby, and Ava . . . for your love, which grows more precious to me with the passing of each year. Also, for being the kind of family where grace is understood and treasured. I'm so grateful to God for the unique way he has used each of you to teach me about him.

PAUL

To my beautiful bride, Susan Ward Gilbert, who suggested over a decade ago that I write a book on the subject of prodigality. Thank you, babe, for ministering alongside of me as we've sought to serve those who have had their hearts broken by a prodigal.

To the Fab Four—Grace, Maggie, Jack, and Virginia Gilbert—I praise God for the way each of you has embraced God's extravagant grace and love in your lives.

To my dad, Kelly Gilbert, for persevering with and loving me through all my years of waywardness growing up. Our history and relationship together made it easy for me to run home. To my mom, Lyn Gilbert, who went to be with the Lord on September 11, 2015: Thank you for the legacy of a changed heart and a repentant life—I love and miss you, Mom.

I'm not sure what protocol prescribes for commending a co-author, but *thank you* Dave Harvey for dedicating the necessary sweat and muscle to bring this project to completion. If it feels like you had to drag me over the finish line, it's because . . . well, you did.

DAVE AND PAUL

To the Elders of Four Oaks, who not only enthusiastically supported this project in spirit, but graciously gave us the time and space to dream and write. A heart-felt *thank-you* goes out to the Four Oaks pastors for their friendship and partnership in the gospel. You men have labored faithfully and fruitfully with the wayward souls that God has placed under your care. Jo LeBlanc, our assistant, did all sorts of "stuff" on this project that no one will every know about—including us!

Thanks to Collin Hansen, Dave Powlison, Robert Cheong, Stephen Altrogge, and Lance Olimb for brainstorming ideas and helping us to think through the concepts of waywardness and rugged love. Thanks also to Brandon Smith, for taking the time to lend his editorial talent to this project.

The folks at Zondervan: you have been simply outstanding! Thanks to Nathan for creating a pretty cool book cover. And a special debt of gratitude is owed to Ryan Pazdur for his vision, personal investment, and gifted editing work on this project.

Jason and Becca and the many others whose names remain anonymous, thank you for allowing us to draw from your stories of waywardness in this book. Your personal testimonies will be an amazing encouragement to all who read this book.

We are indebted to the pioneering work of James Dobson and Dan Allender on the subjects of Tough Love and Bold Love. Their work provided the seeds for our rugged love construct to take root. Paul Tripp, thank you for creating the space in a trial-soaked season to write the foreword for this book. You have served not only us but so many others throughout the world in ways that you will only know in the next life. May God bless your health and push off that next life for many more years!

Is This Book for Me?

Perhaps a curiosity tinted with desperation has delivered you to this book. You want to know whether this book is for you, whether its words can speak to your situation. Maybe you're dealing with a troubled relationship, or someone close to you suffers this sadness. You feel like you need help. You need a friend who can offer perspective and encouragement. You need something—really, anything—that might spark a little hope in your heart.

We understand. We know that time is a precious commodity, and you need to know whether you should spend it with us. So before we dive in, we'll address that question directly.

This book is for you if . . . someone you love or someone close to you loves a person who is rejecting their roles and has stopped listening to the voices of those around them. The situation can be a marriage relationship where a spouse is living in rebellion. The person can be a child who is rebelling against parents. Or a sibling spinning out of control. The person can be a friend or loved one trapped in an addiction, hidden and indulged.

This book is for you if . . . you are struggling to interpret what is happening and how to respond. You don't understand what your loved one's rebellion really means. Is it because of something you've done? Is it a rejection of the truth, a rejection of God? Or maybe it is a mix of all of the above? You wonder, *what have I done to create this mess?* Does it matter if this person claims to be a Christian? Dealing with a wayward person raises questions, complexities, and uncertainties.

This book is for you if . . . you've used every tool in your relational toolbox with few (if any) results to show for it. You've tried communication techniques, confession and prayer, counseling meetings, reading books, talking with friends, and consulting with pastors. You've poured out your troubles to strangers at Starbucks. At this point, you are looking for anyone who might offer help.

This book is for you if . . . you feel like you are running out of patience and are considering the unimaginable nuclear option—*to let them go.* Yet the idea of showing this person the door stirs fears, anxiety, and the dread of losing them forever. You are not sure you can handle the fallout.

This book is for you if . . . you're trying to understand the shame you experience because you loved someone more than they loved you; someone who has abandoned you or used you and has left you with the wreck of a broken relationship.

This book is for you if . . . you feel like this difficult relationship has revealed the worse side of you. You've thought things, said things, *shouted things* that you never believed could tumble from your mouth. You've begun to realize that you are not merely a sufferer helping a sinner. You are a fellow sinner and a former prodigal who still needs grace each day.

We've written this book for those who are weary of serving someone who sucks the life out of you. We know what it's like to deal with the mind-bending, energy-sapping, rest-denying, bone-tired *exhaustion* that accompanies serving someone who is living in rebellion. It takes a special kind of love—a rugged love. It requires a fresh vision for the relationship—a redemptive hope that releases the person to God and trusts in his work when you can no longer be an agent of change. Perhaps you are struggling to see God's hand in your wayward situation. If your vision of God is clouded and you're having difficulty finding faith to go on, *this book is for you.*

We are two pastors with close to fifty years of ministry experience who have thought deeply about this subject and have experienced many of these challenges within our own families. We've written this book because it addresses a topic that rarely makes the seminar list and often remains hidden within the church. We can't promise immediate results, but you likely know that quick fixes are not part of this story. We're not medical doctors qualified to speak on how and where physiology or mental illness affects how people act and respond. That's another book. As pastors and counselors, we offer to step into your pain and confusion and point you to the One who redeems prodigals with his tough, rugged love. God loves the rebel. He loves those who have rejected him. He cares for the wayward person infinitely more than we do. In this book we want to look at that truth and learn to trust that his prescribed path forward is trustworthy.

If you're out of answers and you've cried yourself to sleep, if you long to look more deeply into the Scriptures for the hope, peace, and wisdom that our prodigal-loving God can provide . . .

this book is for you.

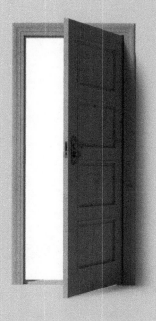

PART ONE

Rugged Life

CHAPTER 1

Break Glass, the Emergency Is Here

The world is broken. But you know that already. Just to get out of bed this morning, you had to dodge the debris. It's why you are here, holding this book, seeking relief from the raining shards of shattered dreams. What kind of dreams? Keep reading, and see if any of these scenes describe your drama.

Jane loved Al, at least the Al she married. But that Al was AWOL and had not appeared in eighteen months. In his place was some kind of teenage twin; a guy who suddenly found the bars and gaming more fascinating than his family. The old Al could be impatient but he listened; he was at least reasonable. This man refused to account for his time or explain why money was disappearing from the bank account.

Jane's friends had stopped calling. No one knew what to say. Attempts to involve their pastor had failed miserably. Al was going rogue. Jane was going crazy. *I'm losing my husband, and I don't know why.*

The stabs came again. Was it fear? Anger? The ache of a soul abandoned by God? Jane didn't know. She only knew it was always present, a constant companion—an emotional prophet foretelling the coming of more bad news.

Three weeks ago, Al said he needed some space. Within an

hour, he left. Three days later, he reappeared as if the family was clueless and untouched by his senseless indulgences. The next day, Al suggested sex, and Jane suggested counseling. Al got angry and walked out saying he'd be back tomorrow. Jane watched him drive off, his rear-window silhouette growing smaller as a curtain of failure closed over her soul.

It makes no sense, Jane thought as she fought back tears, *and I have no idea what to do. How can I possibly reach him if he doesn't want to be reached?*

■ ■ ■

"What's happened to our daughter?" The anguished question came from Meg's parents, both committed Christians, as they poured out what we've come to see as "prodigal pain."

Meg had always been a social sparkplug at church, igniting life among her friends and occasionally even a small but manageable fire. But Meg's life ran pretty smoothly down the tracks laid out by diligent parents and the Christian school she attended.

But last year, Meg jumped the tracks.

It started with a new group of friends, a variety of reckless and unruly teens united by little more than all they opposed. Meg's parents were concerned, but they allowed a little rope in response to her lobbying efforts. Then Meg began to change . . . and not for the better.

First came the lies, more unusual for Meg but hardly uncommon in the world of teenagers. She was caught cheating on a test, then was picked up for underage drinking. Meg's parents put her on lock-down, and that was when Meg the Sparkplug became Meg the Flamethrower.

Meg's dad hung his head, her mom sniffling quietly. I looked away, leaving space for them to breathe, bleed, and decompress. Parents of prodigals live in a world of battle fatigue. Disoriented by the stress and assaulted daily by a nameless enemy, they need time to talk their way forward through the fog of war. My job, at least at this stage, was to listen.

Meg snuck out. Often. When her parents caught Meg returning one night, she was too drunk to respond to their questions. But the change didn't stop at alcohol. There was something else happening—a deeper and darker transformation in her personality. Meg's effervescent temperament had morphed into a sullen, angry, family-hating, talk-resistant rebel. She shrugged off all attempts at advice or care. She said nobody understood her, nobody liked her, nobody defended her. Meg became the consummate victim.

Things were bad. Really, truly bad.

In the weeks that followed nothing worked. Threats, groundings, suspension of privileges, visits to the youth pastor, they tried it all—the Hail Mary pass thrown by desperate parents to gain back lost yards and no points.

Last week, Meg announced she was dropping out of school. Now she spoke of a long road trip with some friends. Meg had a rapid paving project underway, clearing her path straight out the front door and into a world of darkness.

Meg's parents sat before me exhausted, bewildered, and demoralized. It was the lowest moment of their life, and I had a front row seat to their hitting bottom. An indescribable grief owned the moment. Then Meg's mom broke the silence, whispering in a tone betraying a sliver of hope, "This can't be the end of Meg's story, but how can we help her if she won't stay? *How do we know if it's time to let go?*"

■ ■ ■

The chair was empty. Again. It had been five months since Robbie had been to the Bible study. Very few people knew why, but Sean knew. Robbie was not only a kind of spiritual mentor, but also Sean's best friend. It's just not supposed to go this way. Sean rolled the thought over again in his mind, stopping at the same conclusion. He just didn't get it.

But then again, it wasn't rocket science. The new job came, and Robbie jumped on it. Sean didn't blame him—more money, more responsibility, travel, and lots of other perks. But somehow it all contaminated Robbie, as if he had swallowed a poison that polluted his soul.

First came the communication slowdown. Robbie, the guy who always answered on the first ring, started fading back. Then "the girl" appeared. Robbie called her eye candy, which always struck Sean as pretty superficial and demeaning—totally out of character for Robbie. But before Sean could even talk to him about it, the uptown parties started claiming Robbie's Saturday nights. Soon afterward, Sean got bumped from Robbie's social calendar, a second-stringer watching from the sidelines as Robbie's life imploded. It was humiliating.

Not long afterward, Robbie stopped coming to church. Recently Sean heard a rumor that "eye candy" had moved in with Robbie for a more permanent hook-up. But Sean can't get any straight answers—Robbie no longer answers his phone.

Sean stared at the empty chair.

He searched for a word, settling on *flummoxed*. He was freakin' flummoxed. The history they shared said it all. Robbie had been instrumental in Sean's conversion and was there when his parents divorced. Sean felt like Robbie was his brother-from-another-mother, the guy who knew what he was thinking and how to make him laugh, an unexpected gift from his heavenly Father to be enjoyed long into the future.

Now Robbie was gone. Sean's "best friend" wouldn't even answer his calls, much less explain his absence. Sean felt the sting of shame. Friendships—real friendships—were not supposed to arc this way. They had plans to travel together and stand as best man at each other's wedding. Then Robbie just bailed out and pulled the ripcord—no discussion, no explanation, no looking back. Sean felt so betrayed.

How can he just cut me out without discussion or explanation?

Sean knew there was something more significant, more eternal at stake in Robbie's recent decisions. Robbie was fleeing his Savior, rejecting the one who had shown him grace and mercy. And Sean knew that a crash-landing was up ahead. He was no Solomon, but he knew that prosperity and eye candy are never permanent.

"Serves him right."

Sean knew that it was wrong to say that, but he was angry. He felt used . . . and *disposable*. Sean prayed to God for help with his anger and began to pour out his questions.

"Lord, how can I get through to my best friend? Should I beat down his door? . . . give him space? . . . call a prayer meeting? *What does it look like to wisely love one who strays?*"

■ ■ ■

"Prone to wander, Lord, I feel it. Prone to leave the God I love." These lyrics from the classic hymn "Come, Thou Fount of Every Blessing" describe life in a broken world. There is an impulse embedded so

deeply in creation that it even touches God-lovers. It's a feeling that swims against the stream of our profession of faith, a strain of insanity that pushes us to stray from the One we love.

We're prone to wander.

Most of our wandering is, well, pretty routine, even somewhat predictable. We all know that life in this world is not Eden. The world is fallen, broken, and cursed. We live considerably east of the Garden, where fouler winds blow and storm damage is everywhere. We live in a land where marriage is hard, relationships rupture, and saints suffer. A life where we often want more than we have. We envy, or lust, or get angry when things don't go our way. We're not yet what we will be. Life can get messy, and relationships can be painful. But our trials and transgressions seem common to others.

East of Eden, life is never tidy. Sinners sin. It's been that way since the beginning.

But there are times when wrong behavior takes a particularly destructive turn. The saint goes sideways; the soul goes AWOL; the heart grows ice-cold and chills a whole family or church. Our spouse cheats on us, but they don't seem to care. A child rebels, rejecting our counsel and guidance—and runs away. A friend betrays our trust, and instead of apologizing, they don't care.

When someone we love goes rogue and shows *no signs of repentance*, we feel lost. Few things crush the life out of us more than experiencing the remorseless rejection of someone we love.

This is nothing new, of course. Cain was Adam's oldest son—the first kid ever conceived on earth. His mom and dad walked with God. Their first address was paradise. Adam worked in a garden there and enjoyed afternoon chats with the Creator of the Cosmos. But Adam and Eve chose their own way, and their sentence was life in a fallen world, a place where sin now holds dominion and has cursed every relationship. Their relationship with God. Their relationship with each other. Their relationship with their kids.

Sin crouched at their son Cain's door, and forgetting his parents' mistakes, he invited it in to party. Cain killed his brother Abel, and he lived the remainder of his days with a mark to prove it. Adam and Eve—the only parents in history to have known the peace of paradise, the only mom and pop to walk the Garden with God—raised a murderer.

Sometimes people who claim to walk with God, who belong to his church through conversion or upbringing, do despicable things. They make decisions that are contrary to all they have learned. They do the opposite of what they have promised. They make decisions that decimate marriages, betray families, and separate friends. They reject the roles they once appeared to cherish.

Just like King David.

David had an empire, a harem, a loyal army, and God on his side. But he went dark and sought to bed down Bathsheba, the wife of another man. Since her husband was an obstacle, David arranged to have him killed. He called a gangster hit on an honest soldier to indulge his greedy lust and hide his sin.

David didn't just wander off, like a misguided lamb from his pen. Lies. Lust. Deception. Premeditated murder. David careened off the cliff like a possessed pig, carrying those who trusted him all the way to the bottom.

But David's story doesn't end on the shoals. He eventually repented. A prophet loved him enough to speak truth. By God's grace, David responded and then cried out to God for forgiveness. God did forgive him. But David's sinful decisions still caused great pain. A man was dead. A marriage ruined. Trust was broken. David's choices created kingdom-wide consequences that would spill over on generations to come.

Both Cain and David rejected the roles they were called to—as sons, husbands, brothers, and leaders. Both of them had great potential, but they each descended to a place where they ignored the truth, rejected counsel, and abandoned their calling. They could have cared less about who they hurt. One found repentance, but even then, much damage had still been done.

When someone you love chooses to play in the mud, everyone gets splattered. They may, like David, eventually regret it. But from where you stand right now, regret, repentance, even civility, seem like a toxic cocktail to them—a drink to be avoided, not swallowed.

That's where we want to begin, with these bleeding gashes from the hit-and-run you never saw coming; with the relational complexity and daily uncertainty that you feel at this very moment. You don't understand the present, and you don't know the future. All you have are questions.

If you're still reading, you know the questions:

Why is this happening?

What have I done to create this mess?

Why do I feel so ashamed?

What does love look like right now?

If this person is sucking all the life out of me, why do I feel guilty?

These are really good questions, and this book will try to answer them in light of God's truth. But we also want to change the questions so that you experience the grace that comes from gospel answers.

With these thoughts in mind, let's get started.

Popping the Grenade Pin

Judy jerked her head up, the sweat dripping from her forehead. She opened her swollen eyes. *Was it all just a bad dream?* The memory of Doug's words returned, stabbing at Judy's soul. He had said he wanted a separation. He needed time to "think things over."

"Bastard!"

Judy blinked, trying to calm the storm gathering inside her mind. She took a deep breath, wondering if it would help suppress the nausea. The tears just wouldn't stop. She thought, *This is the worst moment of my life.*

Where did we go wrong?

They had conflict, of course. But no marriage is perfect. Doug's new job demanded long hours from him. It kept him out late. Judy assumed the stress and overtime were the source of his fatigue and irritability, the reason he was emotionally and physically distant from the family. Some days, they felt more like strangers than husband and wife. But she held out hope that it would pass and things would get back to normal soon.

Then Judy heard the first rumor: Doug was seen in a bar when she thought he was working. That didn't sound like Doug, so Judy casually brought it up. He exploded. He ranted about his long hours giving him the right to unwind with his friends. Soon after that conversation, Doug stopped attending church because Sunday was his "only day off."

Judy sank deeper into the sofa wishing it would swallow her.

Things quickly spiraled. Judy's world seemed to unravel before her eyes. She began to suspect the unthinkable. *Could there be another woman?* After carrying that fear around a few days, she finally built up the courage to confront her husband last night.

Doug had stared icily at her and said, "I don't want to talk about her, and if you do, I'm gone."

Judy had pleaded with him to stay. She promised him forgiveness. She begged him not to go, if only for the children.

Instead, he walked out the front door.

That was twelve hours ago.

Judy could no longer hold back the tears. She dissolved into sobs that left her gasping for breath. She needed to talk to someone. She grabbed the phone and punched the speed-dial for Kate. Her sister had always been there for her. Kate would know what to do. She always knew what to do. Kate would save her from this free-fall.

Judy didn't realize that she hadn't hit rock bottom quite yet . . .

REBEL YELL

Kate listened to her sister pour out her troubles, piecing together the details between Judy's sobs. She knew that she had no idea what to say. She was emotionally exhausted, and her own mind was preoccupied with the events of the previous night. As a single mom, life was hard enough for Kate. But now her teenage son Blake's erratic behavior seemed to foul each day with ugly encounters.

Blake's recent behavior bordered on bizarre. Kate knew that the body and mind of a sixteen-year-old boy is a cocktail of chemical changes. She figured he would get through this time, just like she did, like all teenagers do. But then came the new friends, a crew of kids she didn't know, guys who seemed allergic to authority.

Blake had changed for the worse. There were lies, broken promises, accusations of cheating in school, suspicions about sexual activity, and fears of alcohol abuse. There was also the possibility of drug use. Her beautiful little boy had morphed from a typical, sullen teenager into a reckless rebel almost over-night. He decisively rejected all her attempts at advice, help, or care. No matter what she did or said, nothing worked. Threats, groundings, suspension of privileges, counseling, and visits to the youth pastor had little to no effect. In fact, Blake talked about simply leaving and hitting the road with his girlfriend. Kate feared that she would lose her son—forever.

Last night Blake blew his curfew, again. The drunken state he was in when he stumbled through the door at 2:00 a.m.—well, it was too much for Kate. She exploded in anger! Blake threatened to leave, but he was too drunk to execute his plan. Instead, he col-lapsed in bed and was asleep, snoring within seconds. At least he slept. Kate spent the night bouncing between frustration and fear, then anger and sorrow.

Now Judy was on the phone, pouring out her own problems. Kate knew her own family was a mess, and she was at a loss as to how to proceed. It seemed like every attempt to lead or draw lines with her son would inevitably lead to his exit from their home.

FOUR CHARACTERISTICS OF A REBEL

When sisters suffer, sisters cry. So Judy and Kate cried together. And as they swapped stories, they began to see some common elements in their relational crises. While Doug's and Blake's destructive choices were different in many ways, their patterns of behavior were remarkably alike. Four similarities stood out to them.

Personal Irresponsibility. Both Blake and Doug seemed to be "off the chain" with personal choices. They were rejecting their roles—as husband and son—and were acting irresponsibly. They showed no sense of accountability to anyone or anything any longer. And this change had left both sisters in shock. It didn't feel real, watching their loved ones make devastating decisions that were so completely out of character. They wondered: *Who is this person? I don't recognize him anymore.* These choices were not just "private" ones that impacted him personally; they had public consequences. They were hurting their friends and family members, leaving behind a trail of broken relationships.

Victim-Centeredness. Kate and Judy were also surprised to find that both Blake and Doug had become incredibly self-focused. They seemed blind and unaware—or unconcerned—about the pain they were causing others. This selfishness was rooted in a story, a narrative they told over and over again where they were the victim, the one who had been hurt. The sisters realized that something truly destructive had taken root. With their loss of personal responsibility, both loved ones had become consummate victims. The story they told themselves and other people was about how they'd been sinned against, how they were the victims of injustice. They had not been loved. They had not been cared for. Their concerns had been ignored. Any attempts Kate and Judy made to counter that narrative were strongly rejected. Even worse, they twisted any attempt to speak truth and used it as further evidence of how misunderstood they were.

A Declaration of Independence. Blake's and Doug's behavior was more than a request for fewer boundaries. It was a declaration of their independence, an assertion of their rights, and a desire to be completely released from any commitments. They were rejecting authority and accountability because they saw their commitments as the very source of their problem. If only their families and loved ones would give them what they craved: freedom from obligation and independence to make their own choices, regardless of the consequences. If anyone was at fault, it certainly wasn't them. They had a right to live their own life, free from obligation.

The Threat of Flight. Both women also shared a common experience of feeling used and manipulated. There was a constant threat behind every interaction—the trump card of leaving the relationship. Blake and Doug knew this was what their family feared more than anything. The threat of leaving became the most valuable chip in the game of manipulation, a piece that each man used to his advantage.

SHARING COMMON EMOTIONS

Along with the similarities in their very different situations, the two sisters also discovered some similarities in the emotions they were experiencing. They did not experience the same emotions in every interaction with their loved one, but these four feelings were common to both of them in their struggles.

Shame. Both sisters were aware of a deep sense of embarrassment about the tragic developments within their families. They knew how these situations are often interpreted by people in the community and the church. Some people had been kind and understanding, but others spoke as if Judy and Kate were at fault. Both sisters had felt the ugly blame of others, and to avoid accusation, they were both tempted to hide what was happening from others. It just all seemed so crazy. The shameful burden they carried kept them from pursuing the help their family most needed.

Guilt. Both Judy and Kate knew the Lord, and they knew that in his eyes, they weren't ultimately responsible for Doug's and Blake's behavior. But they still *felt* responsible. When Doug and Blake ranted and blamed them for being controlling or for holding them back from being who they really were, the sisters knew they weren't to blame for everything. But they still knew they *had* contributed in some way. They were both haunted by the specter of their own sins, their own failures in the relationship. They couldn't shake the feeling that if they just hadn't said that word or blown up that night in anger, they might have prevented these tragic developments. "If only" filled their thoughts. If only they'd been a better mom or wife, more loving and understanding, more patient and kind, more wise and discerning.

Hopelessness. Especially debilitating to Kate and Judy was the feeling that things were never going to get better. This dark place where they now lived was the new reality. They felt like the life they had known was over. They were now living under judgment— some divine penalty for not performing better in their roles. They'd done everything they knew to do, but nothing seemed to work. Nothing seemed to change. Nothing could reach the ones they loved. Prayer seemed useless. And the apparent fruitlessness of their efforts just stoked their unbelief. Not understanding the problem and not seeing any results drew a dark and depressing shade over their hope for the future. Life was bleak. God was distant, and they both felt desperate.

Fear. The primary, constant feeling both women struggled

with was an overwhelming sense of fear. The sisters had invested so much in their families, and they feared they were going to lose their loved ones. The hopelessness they felt fueled their fears. Nothing worked, and doing nothing didn't work either. As they talked, Kate realized that fear was now paralyzing her and Judy from taking any sort of decisive step forward.

But even though they recognized their fears, the sisters still had no idea what to do. What steps could they take?

CROSSROADS

Kate and Judy represent many of the people we've met with over the years. They represent some of our own struggles as well. While we've compressed different stories and struggles into these two relationships, we want you to notice the commonalities that characterize the rebellion of a wayward person and the rejection and pain their loved ones experience.

Kate and Judy have come to a place of desperation, but they haven't arrived there overnight. They've been dealing with these difficult relationships for months, trying everything they know to fix them, to reconcile and bring healing to the brokenness of the relationship. But they don't know how to respond or what to do anymore. Should they continue on as before, attempting to manage an increasingly unmanageable situation? Or should they contemplate something new, bold, or unusual? If they do choose the latter path, what does it involve? Giving an ultimatum? Showing radical forgiveness? Making new sacrifices?

Imagine you're a friend to Kate or Judy. How would you offer them hope? If you were a relative, how would you encourage these women to love?

We ask these questions because they provide a context to

consider an even deeper question swirling somewhere in Kate's and Judy's conscience. A question that speaks to their deepest fear: *What would happen if, having done everything we can, we must simply let Doug and Blake go?*

What would it look like if Kate and Judy released these men to walk in the consequences of their choices? What if they allowed them to taste the fruit of their actions without the security of a safety net underneath their lifestyle? Would this choice be a courageous one or an act of anger and hopelessness? Could it be a loving choice, one made with prayer and counsel? Or would it simply be a chance to dish back some of the pain they had both received? Even if Kate and Judy were set on releasing Blake and Doug—what would that mean?

How will the women know when to let them go?

CHAPTER 3

The Way of the Wayward

Sitting in a front row seat and listening to Kate's and Judy's stories feels a bit like driving by the scene of a terrible car crash. We feel great sympathy for the victims as we slow down to take a look, but we drive on, relieved it's not us. Yet the truth is that none of us are strangers to the moral and relational carnage we see unfolding in these dramas. You may not have experienced the same level of rejection or had a loved one rebel and walk away, but who doesn't have a family member, a friend, or a friend of a friend who has made bad decisions, leaving you to suffer some of the consequences?

Seeing the mess is one thing. Seeing it and giving it a name is another. Before we can find solutions and responses to this "mess," we need to better understand it. In the last chapter, we identified four common characteristics of a rebellious person—a lack of personal responsibility, a victim mentality, an assertion of rights and independence, and a manipulative threat of flight. But let's take a step back and ask some key questions. How do you know when someone you love is ready to boil? What does it mean to be "wayward," to engage in rebellion and throw off responsibility and accountability to others? What defines this person's world? And equally important, how do we engage this person?

WHO ARE THE WAYWARD?

If you want to understand the rebellion of the wayward person, you can start by looking in the mirror. What do we mean by this?

Well, we need to begin with the truth that all of us since Adam, everyone who has ever lived, is a player on Team Wayward. The Bible tells us that we are all born alienated from God with our hearts polluted by sin. We all make sinful choices.

We need to understand that at the root of our sin is a rebellious heart. Our sin is more than just a "mistake" or a "bad choice" or something we would not do if we just knew better. No, at the core of all our sinful actions is a sinful heart that rejects the rule of the King of this universe, our Creator. Instead of bending our knee to King Jesus, we pull him down from the throne and set ourselves up as lord and master of our own fate. This streak of rebellion is the inheritance of every son and daughter of Adam and Eve. We cannot escape it. And it infects everything we feel, everything we think about, and every choice or decision we make.

Wayward is in our blood. Watch a two-year-old kid stand defiantly against his parents shouting, "No!" No one taught him to rebel—it spills naturally from his cute little corrupted heart.

"No!" is in our DNA, factory-installed in our genetic code.

In his magnificent grace that is common to all, God restrains this rebellion. He provides order to our lives by giving us an innate awareness of right and wrong, a broken compass that still provides some sense of direction, even if it can never guide us back home to the arms of the Savior. He also provides us with grace through his revealed law, the Bible, a guide to help us in our deafness and blindness better to hear and see the God who made us to live under his rule.

Yet these gifts, gracious as they are, cannot ultimately change our hearts. They can show us what we must do and what we cannot do, but they cannot fix the rebellion that lies within our heart. To fix that, we need help from outside. We need a new life, a new will, a new desire that loves what is truly good—God—and hates the evil of our sin and rebellion.

Because all people have sinned and gone astray like wandering sheep (Isaiah 53:6), each one of us needs a Redeemer, a substitute who will pay the debt we owe for breaking God's law. This Redeemer is Jesus Christ—the one whose love has the power to break the heart of the worst rebel. Jesus loves the wayward, and he rescues wayward hearts by giving us a new heart—the ability to hear and respond to his voice (John 10:27). Jesus transforms us, calling us to a new identity and role in his kingdom (2 Corinthians 5:17).

So what distinguishes saved sinners from the wayward people we are talking about in this book? The former are *aware* of their sin. They know that they are straying, and they seek out the mercy and grace of Jesus Christ. They *want* to change, but they may be struggling to do so. They are not perfect, and they may sometimes take two steps forward and tumble back a step, like any sinner saved by God's grace. But they display a consistent heart inclination that moves forward toward faith and obedience.

The wayward people, on the other hand, exhibit ongoing, willful, entrenched disobedience. They are committed to a pattern of unrepentant sin. They are not concerned about change. They aren't interested in hearing what you or anyone else thinks. They want people to confirm what they think, what they choose, and do not want to hear a word of correction.

To put it simply, and perhaps directly, a wayward person *is a fool who rejects right voices and renounces true roles.*

THE PRODIGAL AS FOOL

You may find that word *fool* a bit strange, maybe even harsh. Poll folks at your neighborhood Starbucks to define a fool, and you will get as many opinions as there are flavored coffee drinks. A palace court jester or entertainer might be one image conjured up, or perhaps the kid who loves goofing up, or goofing off, or someone who makes very poor decisions.

The Bible has a far more sobering definition of a fool.

Fools say in their heart that there is no God (Psalm 14:1). And no need to be a card-carrying atheist to qualify as a fool. You can believe that God exists but still reject him as the authority over your life. You can be filled with the kind of folly that convinces your conscience that he's irrelevant. Certainly the demons believe that God exists, and they shudder (James 2:19). They do this because, unlike the fool, they take God seriously.

Foolishness is a frightening thing. Proverbs is the go-to book for understanding the profile of the fool (see Proverbs 12:23; 20:3; 29:20). The fool is a person whose heart is bent toward and governed by a dangerous and repetitious refusal to listen to God. A fool ignores God's functional authority. This means that when he or she makes a decision, God isn't in view. In fact, he's barely an afterthought.

Picture a man engrossed in an episode of his favorite TV drama. He suddenly smells smoke wafting in from the kitchen. Fire is serious—something that can destroy his home and his life. To deal with the fire, all he has to do is pry himself from the sofa and pop the pin on the fire extinguisher. But he's too absorbed in his program to be disturbed by the fire consuming his oven. It might be that he loves his leisure, preferring the entertainment of his show, but we all know that the man is acting as dumb as a doornail. His judgment is impaired. He has wrongly weighed his priorities. He has neglected his own protection, making a choice that puts his own life in jeopardy. He's a fool.

Fools will often catch the scent of God's smoke. They have a sense there is a problem. They may have an awareness that they are making a bad choice. But God is a distant fire in a different room, easily ignored by whatever is amusing their heart at the moment. As we saw earlier, at heart a fool doesn't really *want* God's intrusion. He prefers his rebellion and doesn't want to listen to God's warnings. He's too busy entertaining himself. And when a fool decides to reject God's voice, he'll stubbornly and inexplicably allow his life, job, marriage, family, children, and money to go up in smoke.

A PROFILE IN FOOLISHNESS

Ron is a fool. We describe him this way not as an insult but to connect his life with the person described in the Bible. You see, Ron's life has been a slow burn for a while now. Despite repeated warnings from the community college registrar, Ron's academic enrollment was suspended for the spring semester. Ron vaguely remembered that the reason had something to do with incomplete assignments and missed final exams, but Ron always made it a point not to sweat the details.

Ron then found himself out of a job. It seemed his employer had a "three strikes and you're out" policy with punctuality, and Ron didn't even remember the first two.

And then there was life at home, the third circle in Ron's trifecta of foolishness. He and his parents had a deal: he could live and eat at home if he simply paid a modest rent. After a few missed payments and gentle reminders from Mom and Dad, it became evident that home life wasn't a path forward. Ron now found himself looking for a new place to crash.

For Ron, life just sorta happens—he's *that* guy. What defines

Ron as a wayward fool is not his failures per se, but *his refusal to take his fingers out of his ears*. He's sauntering out into the middle of rush hour traffic while friends and family are frantically waving their arms and screaming his name. But Ron is too busy enjoying the Ron-fest to take notice of the eighteen-wheeler barreling straight at him.

The fool thinks he's right in everything he does (Proverbs 12:15). Right up until impact.

REJECTING RIGHT VOICES

Wayward people are not entirely deaf. They hear and respond to many voices. But like a toddler in front of a glazed donut, they're hardwired to dismiss any sounds seeking to redirect them.

You undoubtedly remember the story of the USS *Titanic* and its doomed voyage of 1912. While most know that this state-of-the-art steamship sank from hitting an iceberg, fewer are familiar with the way this terrible accident unfolded. The *Titanic*'s captain and crew might well have saved the ship—and more importantly the 1,500 people on board who tragically perished—if they had listened to the right voices.

In the days preceding the infamous collision with the iceberg, the captain's bridge received no less than twenty warnings from other vessels about the presence of ship-sinking ice. Amazingly, no less than six contacts were made on the very day the ship's hull plates buckled against an immovable iceberg. But instead of listening to these warnings, the *Titanic* churned full speed ahead, even when visibility became poor. The ship's officers ignored the voices of warning and chose instead to listen to those who believed the *Titanic* was unsinkable—until it sank.

Listening to the right voice can make all the difference. If you ignore the truth, it won't matter what you want or don't want. Reality steams forward and always finds us. Sometimes the collision is disastrous.

For wayward fools, the indifference surfaces in a couple of ways. First, wayward people won't listen to or obey God's voice. They reject God as an authority. And they spurn God's grace and care and see them only as an attempt at control. Second, wayward people silence the voices of significant others as well—parents, leaders, pastors, friends, or spouses. Soon, fools have seared their conscience—the God-embedded compass that helps guide our moral decisions also shuts down. Of course, the censure of these additional voices of friends, family, and conscience is just the outworking of the decision to tune God out. When we refuse to listen to God, we grow deaf to anyone who tries to speak the truth to us.

RENOUNCING TRUE ROLES

What happens when wayward people stop listening to God and ignore the counsel of others? *They begin to reject their God-given roles.* So much of what we are called to do in this life finds expression in the roles we fill: as mothers, fathers, daughters, sons, husbands, wives, employees, employers, church members, and the like. The foolishness of a wayward and rebellious heart ripens into rejecting responsibility and accountability to others.

Meet Julie. She used to be a pretty "good" kid who rarely caused her parents any problems. She was a decent student and liked to spend her free time with her friends. Then she met Molly—not the girl, the drug. Now Julie is skipping school constantly and lying to her parents about her whereabouts. Her circle of friends changes regularly, and her social life is a mess.

Recently Julie's song of rebellion hit a higher octave when she was caught stealing money from her younger sister. Then she was suspended from school for some unexplained absences. The situation is deteriorating each day: Julie's parents are infuriated, her sister is devastated, and her school is considering expulsion.

While there are many ways to consider this situation, we find it helpful to look at Julie's relationships and her primary roles in relation to others. If you look closely, you'll find that Julie has rejected and redefined all her primary roles. *Daughter* does not mean what it once did to her. It used to mean a relationship of trust and obedience to her parents; now she sees them as people to use when she needs something. *Big sister* no longer calls to mind the responsibility to model godly behavior and lovingly serve her sibling; it is a lever for manipulating someone who trusts her. *Student* is not seen as a privilege, an undeserved opportunity to learn from teachers and gain valuable knowledge; it is viewed as a serious imposition upon her time in Molly-world.

Let's revisit Blake and Doug, the wayward son and husband from chapter 2. Their situations are the same. They no longer see themselves in light of the gospel story. Instead, they are believing another story, one that puts them at the center as the victim. They no longer see their behavior as sins to be repented of but as expressions of freedom to be enjoyed. Entitlement and privilege have taken root, and the weeds of foolishness are sprouting everywhere. To them, the garden of their heart looks beautiful, but in reality, it is a wild and dangerous place.

Doug and Blake are throwing off the roles and relationships that they have been given by God in order to "follow their heart" and pursue their own selfish desires. They can no longer hear the voice of truth. They no longer believe the story of the gospel, and because the gospel no longer defines their identity, they have lost their way. They are wayward.

You see, wayward is a story believed before it becomes a path trodden. To truly comprehend how voices become muted and roles rejected in the life of the wayward, we must better understand the subversive story they read to themselves. In fact you are about to discover that their behavior is not irrational, but on the contrary is the logical application of the story they believe.

If you're feeling overwhelmed, take heart. You have reason for hope, and that's where we're headed. So keep reading . . .

What the Wayward Want

We have a confession. One of us is a rabid Tennessee football fan. From the time I (Paul) was eight years old, my dad and I traveled 110 miles almost every Saturday to see Tennessee play college football. I never saw a Vols home game on TV—we were always there in person.

Attending the game was a ritual that rivaled church attendance—it was frequent, family-driven, and inspiring. The game itself was often incidental to other game day events. There were the hash browns at Longhorn Diner, the student masses marching toward the stadium, the bookstore visit, lunch at the student union, the postgame tailgating, and plenty of talking on the road. And yes, football. Lots and lots of football. Each win and loss has my father happily ensconced in the memory. Every game reminds me of Saturday afternoons in the autumn gold of Tennessee.

Over the years, I began to see these adventures in a new light. I now realize that my father went to great effort and expense to write a story where I was a principal character in his life. Saturdays and football were just the stage for a drama of friendship my father was crafting with me. It was his weekly attempt at communicating what it meant to love his son. And his investment is now indelibly stamped upon my own soul.

Years have passed, but I can still close my eyes and smell the field at Neyland Stadium. My reminiscence of those days is intertwined with the story of my father's love. And those memories powerfully shape how I think about God and what it means to be a father to my own son. That story shapes how I see myself and how I see the world. My goal is to write a similar story for my own boy—to entrust him with a biography of love in much the same way my father did for me.

Even if he never said it this way, I think my dad understood this. He knew that sharing his story with me in this way would shape and form who I would become. His story would become my story, which I could then pass along to my son. My dad wasn't perfect, but he was discerning enough to understand that *stories shape our identity.*

TELLING A DIFFERENT STORY

Every person has a story to tell. By nature, human beings are story-formed creatures. Our lives make sense to us because we define ourselves in relation to the people around us and the stories we are told. These stories powerfully inform and shape our identity, and over time they define the "roles" we play—the ways we define our relationships to others. Your identity as a son or daughter, a husband or wife, a father or mother—all are shaped by the narrative of your life, your past experiences and the way you view and understand those experiences. For some, these experiences have been in healthy, life-giving relationships, while others have experienced abuse or mistreatment. Who we think we are is largely defined by the stories we tell ourselves, stories that define the way we see the world around us, sometimes called our worldview.

From the beginning, the battle for our hearts has been a fight to get us to believe the True Story. In the garden of Eden, God spoke and walked with Adam and Eve, giving them a role to play in the story of creation. He told them to care for the Garden, to steward his creation, and to live together in loving unity. And the story God spoke to them included a test of obedience: "You may surely eat of every tree of the Garden, but of the tree of the knowledge of good and evil you shall not eat, for in the day that you eat of it you shall surely die" (Genesis 2:16–17). Their role was clearly defined. Every tree was a gift of grace, given for their nourishment and enjoyment—except one. And eating from that tree would lead to death.

The serpent, a crafty fellow, knew that his best chance at convincing Adam and Eve to rebel against God was to change the story. They needed to doubt what God had told them, and in place of the truth, they needed a new story, one that seemed better, more attractive. So the serpent twisted God's story: "Did God actually say, 'You shall not eat of any tree in the garden'?" (Genesis 3:1). Well, of course not. But a seed of doubt was now planted in Eve's mind. In his follow-up, the serpent directly challenged the True Story, telling Eve that in eating the fruit she would not die, "For God knows that when you eat of it your eyes will be opened, and you will be like God, knowing good and evil" (Genesis 3:5). Here is where the story is changed. Instead of death, the serpent tells Eve that eating the fruit will lead to her becoming like God. It's a new story, one that makes her the hero.

Sadly, we know where this story ends. Eve eats the fruit, her husband follows her into sin, and since that day every human heart has been inclined to believe the story that vainly exalts us as the hero. We want our lives to matter, to have significance, but instead of receiving the rewards God promises, we seek our own rewards and believe the story told by the serpent long ago.

This dynamic is what underlies all of our rebellion, all of our wayward wandering, and all of our foolishness. We reject God and the True Story he tells, and we craft our own narratives where we are the victim who deserves something better.

THE WAYWARD WANTS . . .

To better understand this story-corruption, let's further unpack the desires common to wayward people. What is their mind-set, their worldview, and their value system? As we look at this core, we want to explore the patterns, behaviors, and relationships that make up the day-to-day life of a wayward soul. To reach the prodigal, you must first crawl into the story of the prodigal.

Choices without Consequences

Foolish people living in rebellion roll through life like they have a free pass, a "Get Out of Jail Free" card that springs them from consequences. They are constantly dodging the natural repercussions of poor decisions. They follow a risky path, expecting to be bailed out by someone, no matter what black hole they are being sucked into. Over time, their expectation of the "free pass" becomes part of their worldview.

Wayward people want freedom. And they define this freedom as the ability to choose whatever *they want* without the burden of responsibility for their decision. They see their selfish decisions as nothing but "mistakes," so the consequences often strike them as offensive and excessive. Any attempt to connect the dots for them they immediately see as blaming the victim. Their ability to avoid serious consequences reinforces for them the illusion of invincibility, the belief that they can always "beat the rap." In their own mind, they are penalty-immune.

They are just like Blake and Doug.

Doug believed that he could be a playboy and a player, without consequences. Judy challenging him and begging him to stay "for the kids" just poured gasoline on this dream. Blake too believed that his prodigal behavior would elicit little more than a tepid objection from his mom. Kate had rarely drawn firm battle lines in the past. In both cases, Doug and Blake were able to experience choices without consequences, and this experience fed the lies of the story they were telling themselves.

Autonomy without Accountability

We all know that relationships are complicated and defy simplistic explanations. Their success requires us to wisely navigate authority and submission, confession and forgiveness, and rights and responsibilities. It ain't easy! But wayward people want autonomy without the rule of love. For prodigals, maturity means indulging in freedoms, not accepting responsibility. The freedom they want is entirely on their terms. They expect money, liberty, rights, and privileges without standing accountable for what they do with these blessings. They want their dream without any reality crowding in. And the result is disastrous.

Doug and Blake are both believing that they are autonomous and unaccountable in their decisions. They are more than happy to pursue their selfish ways behind a giant veil of secrecy that shields them from voices that might probe or protest. Sadly, these choices sentence Doug and Blake to a life of relational immaturity. If no one challenges them, they are allowed to live in a proverbial bubble—a place where they can freely indulge but never explain. However, raising questions and concerns won't fix the problem, because when anyone who loves them penetrates the bubble, Doug and Blake respond with howls of moral outrage.

That's how the rebellious heart reacts when the voice of accountability violates their autonomy.

Leaving without Loss

Doug wants to pursue another woman while still having access to all the comforts of home. Blake wants to walk on the wild side and still have a safe place to lay his head if he needs it. Both men are indulging in the same desire: to have the safety and stability of home without the entanglement of family, to leave when they want without risking the loss of what they need. Few things launch a family to Planet Dysfunction quicker than supporting a family member in their illusion that abandonment is free.

When wayward people stray from their God-given role, they are banking that everything else in their lives will remain the same. When prodigals perceive that they can wander without the threat of loss, their hunger for sin is fed. This may sound crazy, but in their world, it all makes complete sense. They will do whatever they must to get what they want. That's the nature of our sin—it is irrational, out of touch with reality.

WHEN YOU LOVE THE WAYWARD

When people come to us with their stories of brokenness and pain, they often want to know—why is this happening? What is the cause? Why won't this person listen to me? What leads someone to stray like this, to abandon everything? If you are the one asking these questions, the answer you likely hear and feel most often is—*You!* And that answer delivers daily doses of condemnation.

Even worse, you may be hearing this answer from people you have turned to for help. One of the most virulent strains of legalism within the evangelical church today is deterministic obedience.

This is the oversimplified belief that if I'm a Bible-obeying spouse or a faithful parent, then my marriage will be faithful and my kids will be obedient. Those who believe this have bought into the unbiblical belief that if you live in obedience, God will reciprocate with immediate and discernable fruit. And they believe the opposite is true as well. A weak marriage or prodigal child uncovers patterns of disobedience or sin in the marriage or parenting. If things are falling apart because a spouse is unfaithful or a child is disobedient, you are just reaping what you have sowed.

Sometimes this belief is communicated with a tone of loving concern, but the implication is still there—at some level, you are the one to blame for this mess. One of the most difficult challenges of loving a wayward person is having to bear the burden of others' suspicion. Of course, we're not suggesting that our behavior as a spouse or parent *doesn't* matter. Good parenting does influence children in positive ways just as bad parenting can influence them in negative ways. Same with marriage; a godly spouse can influence the marriage in godly ways (Ephesians 5:25–28; 1 Peter 3:1–2).

In fact, as you begin to think more deeply about your own contributions to the prodigal complexities in your life, you may come to realize that your influence has been great indeed, and not in the ways you would want! This realization that your influence and engagement with the wayward has been laced with your own sin and imperfections can then provide an opportunity for your own repentance and change.

The key word here, however, is *influence*. Too many Christians unconsciously confuse the ability to influence with the power to determine an outcome. They believe that faithfully and obediently honoring your role as a parent or spouse does not merely influence but actually *determines* the outcome of the family. This assumption makes much of humans and seriously underestimates other substantial influences such as God, the world, individual choices, and personal suffering, to name a few.

We're all sinners with the capacity to make choices that take us far from God (Romans 3:23). As we saw in the story of Adam and Eve, a person can have every spiritual advantage yet still rebel against the Creator. People rebel and fall away from God for reasons that have nothing to do with their environment, upbringing, home life, or church family. Everyone stands responsible before God for his or her choices, sinful or not.

But as you begin to ponder your own prodigal problems, you may come to realize that your own contribution has been more than you originally assumed. Sin is like that—cloaking our culpability until God graciously flips on the light. But light always comes with grace, and the clarity on your own contribution carries an incredible opportunity for repentance and change. But for that to happen, we must better understand the problem.

We have noticed that those who love and live with prodigals often follow common patterns of response. The first common pattern is to accommodate and then perpetuate the prodigal's foolishness. So if you see yourself somewhere in what we describe below, don't feel condemned. Every person who has loved others has at some point engaged in unhealthy patterns of relating. It's part of life in this fallen world. More importantly, remember that God is at work right now seeking to rescue you and your loved one. Discussing and understanding these patterns will help you think through how to best disrupt and reorder unhealthy scripts. These are the first steps we must take to change the story the wayward are reading.

Overinvested and Underpowered

Let's begin with how wayward and rebellious people relate to power. Typically, they will seek out more power and control for their lives. Often those who love them unwittingly give in and relinquish their power. This leads to a situation where the wayward people, not the loved ones, are controlling and defining the relationship.

Those who are suffering, like Judy and Kate, often respond in desperation. They do whatever it takes to keep the wayward person from fleeing. They look for a quick solution, something that will produce immediate results. But this behavior reinforces the pattern of the suffering person showing himself or herself to be the one who is fearful of losing the relationship, which in turn puts them at a distinct relational disadvantage. They have little leverage to effect change because they have nothing to negotiate with.

Prodigal sufferers like Kate are often willing to do almost anything to hold on to a threatened relationship. The prodigal, on the other hand, is content doing almost nothing. They have little invested—emotionally, physically, financially—and little incentive to adjust the imbalance. Why would Blake change? He has a pretty good gig, one with lots of personal freedom. And Doug? Well, he has very little "skin in the game," and his relationship with Judy is precariously out of balance. When frantic sufferers desperately pursue the wayward person, the wayward one responds with resentment, scorn, and disengagement. Rebellious fools do not respect fear and neediness. They exploit it.

Enabling and Overresponsible

We see this all the time in relationships: one person overcompensates for the irresponsibility of another person. Instead of allowing nature to run its course, a frantic mom will rescue her daughter and bring the forgotten lunch to her. Doing so occasionally is fine, but when it happens several times a week, it's a problem because the rescuing reinforces bad behavior. Yet more often than not, the mom is bewildered. She can't understand why her irresponsible child continues to leave her PB&J at home! We commonly find a team of enablers encircling the pigsty where a prodigal has settled in. They are ready to sprint into action and clean up the mess when their prodigal has difficulty feeding the pigs. Like the frantic father who insists the training wheels stay on into the child's teen years, those who suffer with wayward fools will habitually rescue them from hazards that could otherwise tutor them. This is a key lesson that we will return to later: *love does not enable sinful behavior.* What we need is not a weak, accommodating "love," but a rugged love, one that allows prodigals to sample the consequences of their bad decisions.

Both Judy and Kate live in fear. Judy is terrified that if she presses too hard on Doug, he will bolt, and she'll be stuck living as a single mom. Yet by failing to confront Doug, she's enabling his behavior and essentially inviting him to keep plodding down his adulterous path. This enabling is a lack of love bound tightly by cords of fear. Kate too has been busy maintaining Blake's "training wheels" to ensure he doesn't suffer a cruel fall. But the harder Kate tries to accommodate Blake's irresponsibility, the more his behavior escalates.

Remember, at the heart of a fool is a tyrant who seeks only his own interest. For Blake, his mom's constant negotiations, pleadings, and threats only reinforce to him that she will always be there to keep him from falling. Why would anyone change that arrangement?

Appeasing and Entitling

Following closely on the heels of habits of enabling and taking responsibility for the prodigal's sinful behavior are the patterns of appeasement and entitlement. When a peaceful country is being invaded, some people respond to the invasion by fighting. Yet others go out of their way to show the invading army that the invaders have nothing to fear from them. *If we do nothing to provoke them,* the thinking goes, *they'll honor our good intentions.* But they are ignoring the far greater reality: they are under invasion!

Prodigal sufferers can be tempted to do the same. Their lives are being destroyed by the sinful behavior of a loved one, but they try to maintain the status quo through bargaining, deal making, and negotiation, thinking that these actions will appease the wayward person. But this situation is not as easy as negotiating a deal at the flea market. It's warfare, and appeasement by the weak only fuels the entitlement of the strong.

Kate is trying to exercise caution and patience in response to Blake's rebellious behavior. Yet her desire to "work with" Blake has emboldened a young man who already feels entitled to freedoms that he has never earned, much less deserved. Like invading marauders being offered water by the defending army, Blake in his adolescent aggression is exploiting Kate's weakness. This weakness is also why Judy never says no to Doug. She *fears* that her enforcement of boundaries will only make Doug more angry and independent. Doug senses Judy's weakness, then exploits her fear to get his way—resistance-free.

LOOKING AHEAD: LOVING THE WAYWARD

We realize that we've raised many questions in this chapter and haven't answered them all. Hopefully, you are beginning to see that there are no simple answers, and often the "obvious" solution is the very thing that enables rebellion. For a person suffering through a situation like this, several questions likely remain:

- How do I begin to change the way I'm acting to wisely speak and push forward in this relationship?
- How do I take steps to disrupt the imbalance of power that currently exists in this relationship?
- How can I begin to restore equilibrium and balance to this relationship with the person I love in a healthy way?
- Is there another, more fruitful way of engaging with them? If so, what is it?

With these questions in view, let's take a close look at what it means to love a wayward person.

PART TWO

Rugged Love

Love Has Teeth—Part I

I f you live with a prodigal, you know what it means to love someone. Love is a means of survival. Love is what gets you up each
morning and inspires you to serve someone who acts like they
hate you. Loving this way means duty, sacrifice, responsibility,
and resilience. Many years back, an R&B icon famously crooned a
pseudo-love anthem to the world asking this skeptical question,
"What's love got to do, got to do with it?" If you live with a wayward
person, the answer is a no-brainer: everything!

But there is a side of love that's difficult to face. You've had a
taste of it already if you are persisting in hope that this person
you love might change. In this chapter, we want to invite you to go
even deeper and join us on a surprising journey that may stretch
your understanding of how to love a sinner who strays.

When people talk about love, they tend to think about feelings of attraction, that joy and excitement of being with someone
who makes you feel alive. However, most of us know that this
attraction is just scratching the surface. Real love is something
deep and powerful, a committed faithfulness that is sacrificial
and loyal. Love is keeping your promises, even when it hurts. It
is patient and kind, gracious and forgiving, and willing to speak
the truth even when doing so is costly (1 Corinthians 13:4–7). We
know this love is tough.

For the most part, this tough love gets us through the tough times. Every relationship experiences struggle. Yet when two people are committed, reasonable, and willing to work things out, love finds a way through it all. But loving a prodigal is even tougher. It's loving a rebel, someone who *isn't* trying to work it out and who *doesn't* have your interests in mind. It's loving someone who is enamored with their sin and does not care about the consequences—the pain and hurt it causes others. As we've seen, wayward fools see themselves as the victim, and they are hellbent on finding their freedom on their terms.

Prodigals need more than tough love; they need a *rugged love*. A love that's bold yet redemptive, forceful yet forgiving, gallant yet gospel-based. Think of it as love with teeth. For prodigals to change, those who love them must exercise a love that is courageous. They need to have conviction and a clear conscience. To love a wayward rebel, you need a rugged love that is rooted in the hope of God's promises.

We offer the term *rugged love* not to pioneer a new way of loving but to bring fresh paint to the portrait of God's unrelenting love in the Scriptures. Rugged love is the way God engages and reaches sinful people. We are all wayward, dead, and trapped in our sin. So the way we love prodigals must be patterned after the rugged love of God.

What is this rugged love? Love is rugged when it's

> strong enough to face evil;
> tenacious enough to do good;
> courageous enough to enforce consequences;
> sturdy enough to be patient;
> resilient enough to forgive;
> trusting enough to pray boldly.

Let's look at each of these six descriptions separately over the next two chapters

STRONG ENOUGH TO FACE EVIL

Bonnie knows Stan is a serial adulterer, but she looks the other way. Walter believes his daughter is on drugs, but he won't probe or ask her questions because he fears the truth. Zoe ignores the cruel and demeaning comments her husband makes about her in public and in front of the kids, hoping against hope that things will improve. Though each situation is distinct and complex, they are all connected by a common compromise: Bonnie, Walter, and Zoe are all tolerating evil. If you ask them why, they say they do it all for love.

When someone you love goes wayward, the worst lies are not always the ones you hear from them. They are the ones you whisper to yourself.

Of course, many of these lies stem from not fully grasping the biblical understanding of love. Our own misunderstandings of what love should look like and how to love others affect our well-intentioned responses to sinful behavior. Wayward people tend to pile up collateral damage like a tornado through a traffic jam. And that carnage of hurt feelings, broken trust, and fractured relationships can be so overwhelming that people like Bonnie, Walter, and Zoe just want to close their eyes and wish it away. They tell themselves that time heals all wounds. If they just ignore it and put it out of their minds, then surely things will eventually get back to normal. They hope to outlive the evil. This lie masquerades as hope, and perhaps on some level, it really is a hope that God will do a miracle. But it's a naïve hope—one that traffics not in reality but denial. And the unwillingness to acknowledge reality only further encourages sinful behavior.

In calling us to biblical love, the apostle Paul says, "Let love be genuine. Abhor what is evil" (Romans 12:9). True and genuine love abhors evil. This means that we loathe and stand in opposition to it. Abhorrence leaves no room for denial. It means that we have eyes to see evil and the courage to respond to it. Sin and folly are inhabiting the soul of the wayward like unwelcome squatters. If these vices are ever to be expelled, they must be honestly named and exposed, not ignored or hidden.

To abhor evil requires a single-minded devotion to accelerating its downfall. The most diminutive mom will strike with ninja speed and nuclear force if she sees a Nazi-loving skinhead threatening her small child. Her abhorrence in this case isn't a mental exercise—"I despise when the strong threaten the weak"—it's abhorrence in *action*, an unwavering commitment to eliminating the threat without hesitation or indecision.

The gospel does not deny evil. The gospel shows us God's response to evil—he abhors it! "For the wrath of God is revealed from heaven against all ungodliness and unrighteousness of men, who by their unrighteousness suppress the truth" (Romans 1:18). God's wrath is his settled and determined response to injustice, sin, rebellion, and evil. He cannot tolerate it, and he will not accommodate it in any way. Christ did not come to earth to paper over our offenses against God. He was not here to spring God free from having to deal with the wickedness of the wayward. The gospel reveals the sinfulness of sin and showcases God's hatred of evil.

God poured out his righteous fury on the only sinless man to walk the earth, who was stapled to a tree on a hill called Golgotha. And not just any man—his beloved Son, who willingly accepted his role as our substitute to free us from our enslavement to sin and reconcile us to God. Ascribed to Christ was our evil—"For our sake he made him to be sin who knew no sin" (2 Corinthians

5:21). Jesus hung suspended, the sacrificial Lamb tarred by our wicked thoughts and actions, and received in his body the full gale force of God's wrath.

Make no mistake; the gospel reveals a rugged love. When we look at this love, we see our sin and our hatred of God and are confronted by the truth that Christ suffered what we justly deserve. The nails were meant for us; the hopeless abandonment and spiritual separation from the love of God that Christ experienced was deservedly ours. God's love, displayed for all to see on the cross, was strong enough not only to face evil, but also to act against it. The cross reveals God's abhorrence in action.

God's response to evil is good news because it has a redemptive purpose, but the path to redemption requires that we come face-to-face with our sin and evil. God's law, given to us in the Old Testament Scriptures, reveals our accountability before God and the rightness of his verdict against Adam and Eve in condemning them to death. Naming our sin and evil is always the first step to experiencing grace and forgiveness. This step cannot be bypassed or skipped. Conviction should lead to repentance, which leads us to forgiveness in Christ.

This gospel is good news because if someone you love is bent on evil, there is help. But repentance is the key that unlocks the power of grace and separates true grace from cheap grace: *But true repentance doesn't come through denial or accommodation.* The pretending must end. The delusion that one can indulge evil behavior with no costs must be exposed. Biblical grace is not a license to sin. As the apostle Paul says in Romans 6:1–2, "Are we to continue in sin that grace may abound? By no means!" It is never loving or gracious to forgive someone simply to accommodate further sin.

Loving like this is not simple or easy. To get here, you need to experience this love yourself, a love so sturdy that it enables you to face your biggest fears—your dread of a loved one leaving you, your anxiety over the unknown, or your unspoken suspicion that this situation indicates you're one humongous failure. Showing rugged love begins by receiving the rugged love of God and holding fast to the promises of the gospel, knowing that our Lord and Savior will never leave us or abandon us (Hebrews 13:5) and that he is truly with us until the end (Matthew 28:20).

Our love becomes rugged as our motivation moves from "peace for me" to "help for them." Rugged love faces human messiness head on. Are you facing the evil?

"Let love be genuine. Abhor what is evil; hold fast to what is good" (Romans 12:9).

TENACIOUS ENOUGH TO DO GOOD

Naming the evil is an important step, but only a first step. Love is made rugged by a tenacious commitment to "not be overcome by evil, but overcome evil with good" (Romans 12:21).

There's an interesting assumption that the apostle Paul makes in this passage. In a cage fight, Paul is saying that good takes evil every time! By doing good—responding with the truth of the rugged love God has shown to us—we overcome the evil that has been done. This point becomes even more important as things deteriorate in our relationship. We need to be ready for the difficult and painful reality that love may require letting a prodigal go. But in letting go, our intent is not to punish the person, to retaliate for the evil they have done to us. Letting go as an act of rugged love is one of the most heartbreaking ways to do good.

There's a delicate period of time, often an extended period, between the early warning signs of prodigal behavior and the decision to let prodigals go. We see their behavior slowly deteriorating, but we may not yet have enough data to plot a clear course forward. We'll talk more about what it means to let go in the next chapter. But at this point, we want you to know this: If you are not taking orders from Scripture, then wayward people's words and actions will set the bar for your response. When they reject you, you will seek to punish them. Their hurtful words will inspire your clever retorts. Everything you do and say will be a tooth for a tooth, and soon teeth will be flying all over the room in an all-out relational brawl.

We must not meet evil with evil. Everyone loses, and you haven't loved the wayward soul. You've merely shown what a more sophisticated drift from God looks like. Doing good requires tenacity because the moments when it's most necessary are the same moments when it's most difficult.

But that's not all that Paul says about this. He tells us that doing good as a response to evil is also an act of subversion. It can have a transformative effect, compelling those who stray to come face-to-face with the truth they have been trying to avoid. "If your enemy is hungry, feed him; if he is thirsty, give him something to drink; for by so doing you will heap burning coals on his head" (Romans 12:20).

The metaphor that Paul quotes from Proverbs 25:21–22 isn't entirely clear, but we can draw one conclusion from what he says: *Doing good to an enemy works good in an enemy.* Commentators tell us that the burning coals may signify shame heaped up by a pricked conscience, or they might indicate the enemy's surprise that you are not returning evil for evil. But one thing is clear: Doing good ignites a burn that supplants the work of an enemy.

As Dr. Martin Luther King Jr. said, "Love is the only force capable of transforming an enemy into a friend."

This was true for Mike.

Mike was a Category 5 hurricane, wreaking havoc and destruction in all his relationships. He was raised in a very loving home by Christian parents, but he chose the path of rebellion. There was no sin he would avoid and no rule he would obey. Mike was a behavioral disaster. He eventually became such a disruptive force in his home that his parents were unable to manage him.

Mike's parents sought counsel, consulted physicians, and attempted every reasonable strategy they could find. After exhausting several approaches, they were left with the heart-breaking step of enrolling Mike in a school for troubled adolescents.

After Mike arrived at his new school, he assumed his parents would just write him off. He didn't even blame them. If he'd been in their shoes, he would have walked a long time ago! But something happened that astonished Mike. His parents did not give up. They launched a campaign of unexpected and persistent kindness.

Mike's parents sent cards, letters, and emails, seizing almost any occasion to mark a moment or remind him of their love. Despite the distance and inconvenience, they never missed a visit and regularly found ways to creatively express their love.

At first Mike thought he was being played. He rejected his parents' love, thinking that they were trying to manipulate him. But their persistence overcame his suspicion, and eventually Mike's heart softened. He began to see them and himself with new eyes.

They never spoke about it, but Mike saw that his parents had suffered greatly because of him. Yet they never seemed bitter! As Mike began to see how self-absorbed he'd become, the guilt stabbed at his soul. Mike couldn't explain it, but even when he was devoted to evil, his parents responded with good. The burn of shame eventually set fire to the rest of his body. The rugged love of his parents was "heaping burning coals upon his head."

As the months passed, Mike started to slowly move back toward his parents. While there was still much to talk about and many obstacles ahead, Mike became convinced that his parents were "for" him. Instead of seeing them as the enemy, he began to understand that they were committed to his good. This kind of assurance empowered Mike to consider his own failures and sin. Coming clean in this way was hard, but his parents' kindness pointed the way toward the kindness of God in the gospel, leading Mike to repentance (Romans 2:4). Returning home would take some time, but powerful forces were now turning the tide in the war for Mike's soul.

When rugged love generates enduring good, it is a subversive and transformative power.

COURAGEOUS ENOUGH TO ENFORCE CONSEQUENCES

Rugged love is a thorough, comprehensive, complete, 360-degree form of love. It's tender when a broken soul needs care and tough when an entitled soul needs to be taken out to the shed. When love is rugged, it's bold enough to define culpability and gutsy enough to expect accountability. A love that lacks ruggedness is only partial love—one that shows up for the party but never sticks around for the clean-up.

True love draws lines. It defines what is good and what is evil.

And when lines are chronically crossed or habitually ignored, true love enforces consequences. These steps, defining right from wrong and good from evil and clarifying the consequences of behavior, are prerequisites for a person to experience the transformative effect of rugged love. The rules and consequences themselves do not have the power to change a person, but unless they are clear and felt, the power of grace cannot do its work.

In Romans 7, the apostle Paul speaks powerfully of the transforming power of God's grace, and in verse 7, he addresses the role of the law in our lives. He writes: "What then shall we say? That the law is sin? By no means! Yet if it had not been for the law, I would not have known sin." Paul makes a convincing case that our only hope of being in right relationship with God is by being reconciled to God through faith in the work of Jesus, who offered himself as the sin-bearing substitute for us. Yet though Paul highlights the saving power of faith over the law, he does not throw the law under the bus. He clarifies the role of God's law *as helping us to first see our need for the grace of God.*

This truth is something that is often ignored in discussions of how to love others and show them grace. What it means, practically, is that the last thing your prodigal needs is for you to prop up their delusion that there are no penalties for destructive behavior. A prodigal needs a love that is rugged enough to insist upon reality. And reality connects consequences to choices.

Nehemiah 9 provides a case study for God's rugged love in action. The Israelites, who by this time had become frequent flyers on Wayward Air, were beginning their journey back toward God. Remarkably, God had never stopped loving them and showing them mercy during their rebellion. Yet the way he demonstrated that love included enforcing consequences:

Many years you bore with them and warned them by your
Spirit through your prophets. Yet they would not give ear.
Therefore you gave them into the hand of the peoples of the
lands. Nevertheless, in your great mercies you did not make
an end of them or forsake them, for you are a gracious and
merciful God.

NEHEMIAH 9:30–31

God first gave Israel his law and clearly stated the consequences for disobedience when he made the covenant with
them at Sinai. He had been patient, bearing with his disobedient people for many years, constantly calling them back
into fellowship and warning them of the consequences through
the prophets and miraculous signs. But as is the case with most
prodigals, what he did was not enough. So God applied the rod by
allowing Israel to be conquered and deported from their home-
land. He held them accountable for not listening or obeying.
God allowed them to experience the consequences of throwing
off his redemptive, sanctifying love. Israel experienced a rugged love!

One father dealing with a wayward daughter—who would
not keep any agreement they made, or curb her hostile behavior toward the family, or stop threatening to flee—said to us,
"Eventually I had to realize that my vision for love was too small.
It was confined to what I could control. If she stayed at home,
my wife and I felt less anxious. But for some strange reason,
the home had become this humongous stumbling block for her.
Eventually we became convinced that we needed to show her a
love courageous enough to impose consequences. So with tears
in our eyes, we asked her to leave."

This family learned there are times when rugged love includes the need for a hard reset—where a forced exit and change of environment creates space for the prodigal child, spouse, or sibling to make choices or live out their worldview. The comfort and security of home buffers some prodigals from the consequences of their choices and leaves essential questions unasked. God's discipline of Israel had the long-term redemptive goal of knocking loose the scales from their eyes. In the same way, the father quoted above realized something critical to moving forward with his daughter: Allowing her to bear consequences did not deny his love for her, but embodied it.

God's mercy is freely given when a repentant heart asks for it, but casting pearls before swine will cheapen them (Matthew 7: 6). Fools in their rebellion will exploit mercy shown to them if it is unaccompanied by cost or consequence. We must never assume that mercy is without cost. The gospel reminds us that God's mercy toward sinners was not free—it was a cost borne by Christ, who paid the price for our sin by satisfying God's wrath. He was crucified so that we might receive mercy. Make no mistake; mercy has a steep price.

That's not to say that we extend grace in a manipulative way. We are simply saying that we need a nuanced response to the complex motives of the human heart. The best way to serve a prodigal husband, sibling, or child is to insist they live in a world where sowing results in reaping and choices have consequences. Underlying our willingness to show mercy and extend grace should be the reality of a world where sin has consequences and repeated patterns of sin lead to destruction. "In order to repent," says Dan Allender, "prodigals must feel pain."[1]

WRESTLING WITH RUGGED LOVE

The car company Jeep promotes their Wrangler model as "rugged." It's built to go off-road, into the hard places of the earth where it needs to withstand a beating from rocks, potholes in the dirt, torrential rains, climbing miniature boulders, and slicing through mud or snow like a hot knife through butter. In a sense, it's built to not only take a beating, but to dish out consequences on whatever comes its way.

Rugged love is a wrestling match with the boulders and potholes of life with a prodigal. Loving your prodigal will often feel like climbing a mountain in an avalanche. But through Christ, you are prepared and built to be rugged—to not only take what comes, but to respond to the terrain.

Let's face it—anyone embracing rugged love faces huge emotional hurdles. It feels like we are piling on, like if we saw a drunk fall down in the street and decided to go over and kick him to teach him a lesson. But if we're serious about helping people enslaved in deep patterns of selfishness, we will find faith to think honestly and deeply about the gracious grit of real love.

So take a breath and keep reading. Doing so could make a dramatic difference in the life of the one you love.

Love Has Teeth—Part II

Neither of us have ever participated in an Iron Man Triathlon, which is instantly evident to anyone who has seen us. Despite our lack of personal experience with this event, we've been told that completing the grueling two-mile swim and the taxing hundred-mile bike ride, as difficult as those are, are just the beginning of the pain. Iron Man participants must push past their weariness and muster strength to tackle the final, seemingly impossible leg: the twenty-six-mile marathon run. It takes a unique kind of internal fortitude, mental toughness, and physical endurance to be certified crazy enough to finish.

Showing rugged love to a wayward person can often feel like you are running a long, difficult triathlon. It requires otherworldly stamina. After finishing the last chapter, you may be saying to yourself—"What, you mean there's more?" You've just finished the two-mile swim—facing evil, doing good, and enforcing consequences—only to find that you must bike another hundred miles up a mountain of relational pain and difficulties.

No, the race isn't over yet. But this is good news.

We say it's good because showing someone rugged love isn't a strategy you employ to guide a prodigal toward right thinking. Rugged love is a means of grace. It is the power of God that enables you to compete and complete this contest. The love we're talking about is eternally durable and otherworldly. When Paul describes it in his letter to the Corinthian church, he says, "Love never ends" (1 Corinthians 13:8). Even if your faith and hope are gone, God promises that love will last. It will win the race (1 Corinthians 13:13).

STURDY ENOUGH TO BE PATIENT

For an eight-year-old boy, Christmas gifts can seem more important than the air he breathes. But when as adults we look back at those childhood gifts, the gifts that seemed so essential at the time—the G.I. Joes, baseball cards, and that truly "boss" Schwinn bicycle with sissy bars, a banana seat, and stingray handlebars— are no longer useful. As the boy grows older, a day comes when these gifts are no longer necessary or beneficial for him.

The Corinthian church was impressed with itself. The people saw themselves as spiritual and mature. When a Corinthian Christian looked in the mirror, he or she saw an incredibly gifted person, someone whose gifts set them apart from the rest. The Corinthians believed that heaven had arrived on earth whenever they gathered.

When Paul writes to these Christians, he agrees that God's spiritual gifts are pretty amazing, but he reminds them that the gifts are temporary (1 Corinthians 13:8). Like the gifts of childhood, they can seem utterly essential, but a time will come when their usefulness ceases. However, one gift of God will never cease—the gift of love!

Paul, in his first letter to the Corinthians, describes this love. And the first word he uses to define the durable gift of love is a startling one—"Love is *patient*" (1 Corinthians 13:4). What does it mean for love to be patient? *When love is patient, it means it is forbearing.* Forbearance is an uncommon word, something you'd hear from the lips of an earnest Puritan. Yet it is a beautiful word that is filled with rich, redemptive meaning. Forbearance is a willingness to patiently bear with sinful behavior *without withdrawing love.* It reflects a love so sturdy that our heart to serve a sinner is not severed by their sin.

When people sin against us, particularly when those we love sin blindly and repeatedly against us, our first instinct is self-protection. We immediately want to withdraw our love and close the emotional gates to protect our heart from hurt. We want to remove ourselves from the line of fire to escape the artillery they launch against us. As parents, pastors, spouses, and friends, we are both familiar with this impulse—the desire to shut out family members or friends who persist in sin. But God calls us to another way, to "walk in a manner worthy of the calling to which you have been called . . . with patience, bearing with one another in love" (Ephesians 4:1–2).

When love is patient, the heart becomes vulnerable to harm. C. S. Lewis once said, "To love anything at all is to be vulnerable. Love anything and your heart will certainly be wrung and possibly broken. If you want to be sure of keeping it intact, you must give your heart to no one, not even to an animal."[2] We don't need patient love when people treat us well. We are less vulnerable to the risk of harm in relationships like this. But what about those who do not appreciate our sacrifices, who sometimes feel like a weight or burden, who do not return our kindness? What about those who don't change and who persist in their sinful patterns and habits?

A forbearing love does not demand a proportional response from those it serves. Forbearing love does not carry a ruler around, always measuring the investment it is making and comparing it to what the one loved is giving in return. Forbearing love does not judge quickly (Luke 6:37), nor does it affix labels to justify emotional withdrawal. A forbearing love is tender, cultivating an open heart toward the wayward, yet holding to the truth and enforcing consequences necessary for the wayward's progress. A forbearing love may even let go and release the person to the life of sin they have chosen. Yet it stands ready to run down the road with open arms to receive the repentant sinner.

Recently I (Dave) was speaking at a marriage conference. I met with a group of leaders and wives, and their first question was about something I had written in a marriage book several years ago on showing mercy in marriage. In that book, I shared the extraordinary story of a courageous woman who showed forbearance toward her emotionally cruel and adulterous husband. She was a truly remarkable woman, and I was honored to include her story.

The couples had a question about something I had omitted from the book. I had focused the story on the enduring patience the woman had shown, but I had neglected to mention that when someone we love is caught in a longstanding and entrenched pattern of destructive behavior, forbearance is more than "sucking it up" and overlooking the offenses. We talked about how true mercy shines God's light on sin, exposes the damage it causes, and trusts God to work through consequences. Looking back on what I had written, I realized that I should have included more of what we're talking about here, that God's love came to us through the cross not by ignoring justice but by satisfying it. True mercy is not motivated by fear. It frees us to identify truth, uphold righteousness, and enforce consequences. Mercy does not enable folly—it confronts it with love and concern for the person.

This raises yet another facet of patient love described in 1 Corinthians 13:4 that is necessary when we are serving one who strays. *When love is patient, it is also honest.* Patient love is not just about waiting it out and being longsuffering. It does not accommodate sinful behavior to the detriment of the sinner. Rugged love should not make us spineless Christians with no taste for truth. On the contrary, Scripture shows us that rugged love is a love with teeth!

We see this patient, rugged love when Paul speaks to the Thessalonians. "And we urge you, brothers, admonish the idle, encourage the fainthearted, help the weak, be patient with them all" (1 Thessalonians 5:14). This passage envisages several different types of strugglers—the idle, the fainthearted, and the weak. But look carefully again at how we are to treat these strugglers. We are called to "admonish the idle" even while we remain "patient with all." The need to admonish someone does not include dispensing with patience, as if the two are in conflict. Being patient with a sinner does not mean that we are blind to their sin or that we ignore the things that need to be corrected.

Love does not accommodate destructive patterns of sin in the name of patience. Yet patience for the idle looks different than patience for the weak. For the idle person, patience requires persistent correction; for the weak, patience shows compassion. Patient love may require that we exercise necessary discipline and speak truth that a person does not want to hear. Yet this kind of patient love should mark our conversations in such a way that it shapes the heart attitude from which we share our words.

Before you jump to showing someone the door, you must carefully evaluate your actions toward the prodigal. Have your attempts to love included unmitigated honesty? We're not talking about turning every conversation into a correction-fest, where you revisit all of your concerns for their soul. But often a silence echoes between the walls of the wayward and those who love them. Sometimes relationships have an unwritten house rule: keep peace, avoid truth. But silence like this is not loving; it is selfish.

"*Selfish?*" you say. "Who has time to love themselves, *or even think about themselves*, when this fallen creature I serve occupies all of my waking hours?" If you'll give us just a moment to explain, this next point may be particularly helpful for you.

When we love people who reject our attempts to love them, their behavior lays the groundwork for something in our hearts that the Bible calls the "fear of man" (Proverbs 29:25). In few places is the fear of humans more prominent, more of a daily battle, than among those who love people who reject their love. Our unrequited love creates a snare for us because it stirs powerful desires in our heart to seek approval from people rather than from God. This desire for approval can lead to exaggerated fear of being rejected by our prodigals, causing them to grow big and God to shrink.

When being loved by someone becomes more important than being honest with them, our fear corrupts the way of patience and forbearance, and we are silent. Seeking temporary peace with our loved one replaces pleasing God. If you're wondering whether all this describes you and your relationship, ask yourself the following questions:

1. *Have I been honest and specific with my pastor and trusted friends about the extent of sinful behavior and waywardness in this situation or relationship? Have I sought counsel on*

how to proceed? The "fear of man" can make us overly sensitive to how our prodigal makes us appear to others. We may be tempted to dismiss or spin their behavior so it doesn't reflect poorly on us.

2. *Have I explained to my loved one that God's idea of love—and therefore my application of love—includes consequences for sinful behavior?* This question does not assume that the wayward care about what you say or that they understand it and believe it. It only asks if you have been honest and clear with them.

3. *Does my loved one understand where I disagree or why I'm concerned because they have heard my view directly and honestly from me?* Fear can lead you to recruit others to communicate the hard words that our loved one should hear directly from us. We are not discouraging you from seeking pastoral or professional help, but this help should be supplemental to your own truth-telling and not a replacement for it.

4. *Have I specifically defined the consequences of engaging in behavior that I believe is most damaging to my prodigal or to our relationship?* Have you made at least several attempts to clearly communicate not only your love, but your specific concerns over the behavior and the steps you are willing to take to get help or see change?

One final characteristic of patient love is the most important of all. *When love is patient, it means Jesus.* The love descriptors in 1 Corinthians 13 are not Paul's attempt to get us thinking outside the box on love. He's not just making these up to be countercultural. He has something—someone—in mind as he shares these qualities. Each feature of love's definition was embodied in the person of Jesus Christ. Jesus was not simply patient but perfectly patient. He was not just kind but flawlessly kind. As love incarnate (1 John 4:8–10), Jesus bore all things, believed all things, hoped for all things, and endured all things (1 Corinthians 13:7).

Jesus, the man of patience, not only embodied the full beauty of patient love, but he adopted a patiently loving disposition toward his own prodigals. Paul told the Romans, "Or do you presume on the riches of his kindness and forbearance and patience, not knowing that God's kindness is meant to lead you to repentance?" (Romans 2:4). Christ's patience has a purpose—to lead to our repentance. Jesus is not patient with us because it is a nice thing to do, a random or arbitrary act of kindness. His love has an intention—to lead us back to God.

We often think about this truth when we reflect on our own lives prior to Christ. We were wayward sinners: creative, determined, selfishly indulgent, and happily blind to the results of our behavior. We were prodigals, wreaking havoc in the hearts of those who loved us. But Jesus was kind and patient with us. At the appointed moment, we saw his love and his enduring patience. We caught a faint glimpse of the many times we had deserved but did not receive judgment for the evil we had done. Jesus' love was not a generic blur of good feelings; it was remarkably captivating, drawing us back to the Source. It spoke honestly to our sin and then waited for our repentance.

RESILIENT ENOUGH TO FORGIVE

If you have ever loved a prodigal, you know what it feels like to be sinned against. A wayward soul stays afloat by cutting away the ballast of concern for other people's feelings and interests. And when they do, things get pretty nasty.

Perhaps the best biblical example is the story of the wayward, prodigal son. You are probably familiar with the story told by Jesus in Luke 15. A man has two sons. The younger son asks his father for his share of the inheritance, a request that in his culture and time was as good as telling your dad you wished he was dead. The prodigal son asking his father for his inheritance was an audacious display of naked selfishness (Luke 15:12). The dad wasn't even close to dead, but the son wanted his cut.

This situation is a great snapshot of living with a prodigal. They wound; you bleed. Pain is a constant companion. How do you keep from collapsing under a weight of resentment?

Rugged loves forgives. Often. Not to keep peace or appease prodigals, but because it sees its own greater debt to God wiped clean. "Be kind to one another, tenderhearted, forgiving one another, as God in Christ forgave you" (Ephesians 4:32).

The path to forgiving lies in considering the astronomical, unpayable debt that God has forgiven us. Because he loves, God forgives. If we love, we'll follow him and forgive too. We see the father demonstrate this type of love as we continue looking at the story of the prodigal son in Luke 15.

When the son asks for his inheritance, his father gives it to him, and the son leaves home for a far-off land where he squanders the money in reckless living. When a famine hits the land, he has nothing left and finds a job feeding pigs. His foolish rebellion has literally led him to the pigsty, rolling in the mud of his sin. He feels the consequences of his choices in the clothes he wears, in his empty belly, and in being forced to eat the scraps he feeds the pigs to survive.

No one helps him (Luke 15:16). But in that place of being alone and without help, a ray of truth breaks in upon his heart.

Jesus tells us that he "came to himself"—something every prodigal must experience (Luke 15:17). He remembers the good life he left at home and contrasts it with the consequences of his choices. And he sees that he has sinned. He responds, "I will arise and go to my father, and I will say to him, 'Father, I have sinned against heaven and before you. I am no longer worthy to be called your son. Treat me as one of your hired servants'" (Luke 15:18–19).

Here we see true repentance. Notice that it happens when the son recognizes the false narrative he has been believing. He acknowledges that what he has done is more than a mistake—it is an act of sin and of rebellion against his father. He recognizes that he is not the victim here. He is "no longer worthy." This awareness leads him to see his role in a new light. He does not feel the right to assert the privileges of a son. He plans to ask his father to treat him as one of the hired servants—even as a slave (Luke 15:19).

You likely know how this story ends. Even as the son is still approaching the house, his father sees him and runs to him, embracing him and welcoming him home. While Jesus wants us to learn much from this story, one powerful lesson is that we must be ready to forgive when a prodigal returns home.

Yet before we put ourselves in this story as the welcoming father, we need to see that every one of us have been the prodigal. We have all left home, squandered our inheritance, and need to repent before we can truly return home. This is your story, and it must be one that you understand and believe before you can live it out like the father in relation to your own prodigal. Are you willing to pass the forgiveness you've received from God along to the one who has hurt you?

The war had finally ceased in the Fletcher household. Two

years of dealing with a runaway, drug-addicted son had inflicted heavy losses on the family. The arrests, school suspensions, late night emergency room visits, and eventually the theft of family heirlooms were all part of the extensive casualty list that had inflicted deep injuries on this family's relationships. Eventually, their son had left. And as painful as it had been to let him go, at least the daily drama ended.

But no one could have predicted what would happen when their prodigal came home.

Despite the fact that they were still hurting and healing from two years of relational combat, the family had fought *for* him rather than with him. Their conversations with their son did not ignore their own hurt and pain. But the family also sought to speak words of love, encouragement, and hope for God's purposes in this young prodigal's life. Freely and joyfully, they released the claims that bitterness and anger sought to make on their own hearts. It wasn't easy, and there were plenty of stumbles along the way. But by the grace of God, the Fletchers were empowered to exchange vengeance for forgiveness. If you asked the family why, they simply said they were following the example of their Savior.

The Bible makes it clear that forgiveness is a two-way street, meaning if we want to receive forgiveness from God, we must be willing to pass it along to others (Matthew 6:14–15; Luke 17:3–4). Forgiveness comes with a redundancy clause attached to it. If we want it, we must share it (Mark 11:25). How do we do this? The cross relieves us of our bondage to enforce punishment for smaller debts by leveling the playing field. The cross reminds us that God has forgiven us an incomprehensible debt. Because of his astounding love, God now sends us to one another to pass along not the punishment but the blessing we've received. Before we can play the role of the welcoming father to our prodigal, we must recognize our own waywardness and acknowledge the grace we have received from our heavenly Father.

In extending grace, we are not the arbiter of penalties; we are debtors who have been forgiven a great debt. We forgive because we've been forgiven with a resilient, cross-bearing love.

TRUSTING ENOUGH TO PRAY BOLDLY

As we have seen, the ability to show rugged love to others is not something that comes naturally to us. It's just not in us to love our enemies, to forgive those who have wronged us, to confront sin and speak the truth while remaining willing to show mercy to those who repent. This love does not come from within us; it is a gift of God, the fruit of his presence abiding in our lives. It is a work of the Holy Spirit made available to those who call upon God in prayer.

Prayer is God's gift to us. It's where our desperate needs meet his faithfulness. This means that prayer should occupy a crucial place in the hearts and minds of those called to love the wayward. Rugged love demands bold, audacious praying that honors God. Through these prayers, God touches the hearts of prodigals and prodigal sufferers alike.

We see a biblical example of this type of prayer in the story of Hannah, an Old Testament believer who knew the disappointment of unfulfilled dreams. Though Hannah wasn't wrestling with a wayward son or daughter, she was in a place of deep sadness and despair. She could not conceive a child, and while baby showers were happening all around her, Hannah's womb was empty. Her heart was filled with grief and heartache (1 Samuel 1:6, 10).

Does the pain of having *no* child really compare to the pain of having a *wild* child? It might be helpful to immerse ourselves in Hannah's world for a moment. Being married with no kids three thousand years ago in Middle Eastern society was a mark of shame, an identity defining reality that was permanently etched on the barren woman's soul. Hannah's shame was so great that she stopped eating (1 Samuel 1:7). Her grief replaced food as her daily meal.

Maybe you can relate not to Hannah's barrenness but to her grief. To her sense of impotence and despair. Like Hannah, you look at your family, and you know something is missing. A work of God is desperately needed.

We can learn from Hannah because like her, we must come to embrace certain undeniable realities. First, *Hannah came to see that her situation was God's choice.* Her plight was not happenstance; it was under the complete care and control of her heavenly Father. Nothing was happening to Hannah outside of God's loving plan for her life. Second, *Hannah could not repair the problem.* There was no way she could jumpstart conception. There was no pill to take or treatment to follow. And if there were, she had likely tried them all. Underlying her physical barrenness is a deep awareness of her spiritual barrenness. Like Hannah, we too must recognize that we simply do not have the power in ourselves to create spiritual life. Left to ourselves, we are powerless to change the wayward heart.

But this is not the final word for Hannah. In her powerlessness, *Hannah had to trust God.* Through the unexpected grace of a barren womb, Hannah learned to trust God completely with what she could not comprehend or change herself. Hannah's desperation became an invitation to meet God through her honest, bold, and audacious prayer.

Listen to Hannah's prayer as she walks through the valley of death, pouring out her heart to the Lord (1 Samuel 1:10–15). Her faithful prayer in a time of deep need can serve as a model for our own.

"*I am a woman troubled in spirit . . . pouring out my soul before the Lord,*" Hannah told the priest who questioned her (1:15). Hannah didn't keep her pain locked inside. She went before God, crying out to him with tears, moans, and cries of pain. And God listened to her. He will listen to you too. The Lord turns no one away who sincerely seeks him, even when we are profoundly troubled. (See Psalms 6; 18:1–19; 118:5; John 12:27–28.)

"*O Lord of hosts, if you will indeed look on the affliction of your servant and remember me and not forget your servant, but will give to your servant a son, then I will give him to the Lord all the days of his life*" (1:11). Hannah's prayer is honest, direct, specific, and sacrificial. Hannah knew God was behind her barrenness. So she turned to him for help. Confess your complete inability to change the wayward heart of your loved one, and confess your total dependence upon God for this transformation. Declare your willingness to trust him, even when you see no evidence of new life. Pray like Hannah specifically and boldly about what you want God to do in the life of your prodigal. Pray for God to arrange circumstances, situations, and people to spark change in the heart of your loved one. Like Hannah, pray for life!

"*She continued praying before the Lord*" (1:12). Hannah persevered in prayer. She came back to God over and over and over again. Then she prayed yet again. Follow Hannah's example. Don't give up, and don't shut up. You express your humility and dependence when you repeatedly come to him in prayer. Read

Luke 18:1–8 and ask God to make you persistent in prayer. When you grow weary, ask a friend to help you by praying with you.

We know that many people have probably encouraged you to pray about this relationship and to bring this situation before the Lord. And to be clear, we aren't suggesting that prayer is a magical formula that suddenly makes everything easy. Your situation may not improve. The person you love may not change. But the Spirit works in us and through us as we come before God in helpless dependence. He works in those times when all we have are tears, when we can only speak in groans of pain and have no words to express our suffering. He works as we come back to him again and again and turn to his promises as the defining reality of our lives. Even when everything screams out that we should give up and the situation seems hopeless, we need to remember that apart from God, we are all hopelessly lost.

Our own salvation is a miracle of grace, and when we need a miracle, we are not asking for something unusual. God specializes in miracles. They are often how he does his best work. This is why we pray for them.

LOOKING AHEAD: LOVING BY LETTING GO

Coming to terms with what makes love rugged sends us down the road on our journey of loving the wayward. But as difficult as all of this sounds, we haven't arrived at the most difficult application of rugged love. If you made it this far, it's probably because you need help and other approaches have failed. Don't be discouraged. God loves you, and he loves your prodigal more than you can possibly imagine.

What does it look like when you begin to love ruggedly and the person does not respond or repent? Everything you can try you have tried . . . and then tried again. You feel like your relationship is a Cold War with no thaw in sight.

Earlier in the chapter, we mentioned the idea of a hard reset, a seemingly audacious act of love. In the next chapter, we'll look at what it means to show rugged love in one of the most difficult ways possible—by letting the person we love go. Sometimes loving someone means letting them suffer the full consequences of their choices. It's never easy, and there's no guarantee they will return. But there are times when it's the most loving thing we can do for them.

CHAPTER 7

Pursuing the Wayward

W hat should I do now?"

The question hung in the air, suspended somewhere between desperation and hopelessness. James, a man with a big heart, was emotionally fried and utterly lost. Lucy, his wife of twenty years, had just announced that she was moving out and had designs for a better life.

"I'm unhappy," she said. "My hope is gone, and I don't want to be married anymore. I need to create my own life, independent of you."

O God, can this really be happening? James felt like he'd blinked twice, and their marriage had gone from honeymoon to Hades.

Part of James didn't blame Lucy. He knew he worked too much and was too invested in sports, football being his drug of choice. It seemed like he and Lucy never talked anymore, aside from the business-like drudgery of deciding how to pay the bills or planning the kids' transportation to games and recitals. As for romance—James would be the first to admit that they lost that lovin' feelin' years ago.

Still, James assumed things would get better, not worse. But worse came with a vengeance—Lucy's slow disengagement from life at home. The drift was undeniable. He tried to be understanding, but his kindness just seemed to embolden Lucy.

James's plan took shape as Lucy was upstairs packing. What

she needed was greater forbearance and unconditional love, he told himself. It would be hard, but he would forgive her. Then he would double-down on mercy—he'd promise to change, call the pastor, ask that she stay for the children. He'd even plan an immediate romantic getaway! The main thing was that Lucy had to stay; he needed her to stay!

But before he could pitch the plan, the front door slammed. Lucy was gone. No matter, James would find her. If nothing else, they'd have to talk about the kids. He would never let go. James knew love never fails, which means it never lets go.

Maybe you can relate to James's story. Many can. Your teenager is rebelling; a friend in your small group has left home; or your spouse has been caught in some sort of illicit addiction. The absurdity of the wayward world has invaded your life, and like James, you are asking, "What do I do?" As we discussed earlier, the initial impulse in dealing with those who are straying is to pursue, plead with, or strike a bargain. It seems so right, so natural, so . . . biblical! However, something that feels so right can often be stunningly misguided.

To help us unpack this issue further, we want to consider two questions: First, what's the goal or "end game" when engaging those who stray? Second, what are the means God uses to change wayward hearts? Tackling these questions will help us begin to reorient our approach to people we love when they make relationally destructive decisions.

THE END GAME: A CHANGED HEART

After absorbing the initial shock of Lucy's declaration of independence, James began to consider his next steps. In all honesty, he would have been relieved to simply have Lucy renounce her drift, recommit herself to the marriage, and move back home. After all, Lucy's actions were causing deep anxiety for James and disrupting every dimension of their family life.

We get that. Who can't be sympathetic with James's desires for normalcy and a return to matrimonial stability? However, James's impulse to sacrifice almost anything to restore the marital equilibrium fails to ask a more important question: What does Lucy really need? What's going on in her heart that has fueled her flight from God and her marriage? What does loving her really look like right now? When we ask these frightening but courageous questions, the "end game" comes into focus.

Simply put, our desire for those who stray is that they encounter gospel realities in our response. We want to set a full table of God's love and forgiveness for them, not just the sugary dishes of sentimental love or misguided forbearance. This is a more robust and courageous love, a love willing to draw lines because it sees a bigger picture. Robert Cheong describes our proper goal: "God calls us to pursue, encourage, and warn one another in the midst of our sinful struggles in ways that reflect how He mercifully deals with us. The goal of such pursuit is for the wayward ones to repent of their sin and turn back to Jesus, experiencing His restoring love (Isaiah 55:6)."[3]

When people you love embrace contradictions and act irrationally, they shovel chaos into the lives of those who love them. We react by reaching for peace at any cost. Let's face it: loving a sinner who strays is exhausting! We can find ourselves negotiating for behavior that simply manages the sin so that everyone can survive. In the upside-down world of reaching a prodigal, this response makes complete sense. It certainly did for James. But as difficult as it may be, true love always has an eye on the end game.

If James only wants behavioral changes in his wife, he's missing the end game. Lucy has a God problem. Her departure from James is quite serious, but it mirrors a deeper and more profound flight from God. Thus, her patterns of sin provide a window for James (and others) to engage Lucy's mind and soul.

Band-Aids won't help. Lucy has been slapping those on for years! She now has questions about meaning, trust, and fidelity that can only be answered by Someone Divine. Her greatest need is *not* within her marriage. This doesn't mean that real, practical problems aren't being generated from her spiritual chaos—there are! But prodigals will push you toward pragmatism at the very time they need a Big God. Remembering the end game—seeing our prodigal restored to Jesus—is our only hope.

THE PREGAME: REDEMPTIVE RELEASE

James attempted to win back Lucy's love by doing what seemed natural and humble: he took the blame for Lucy's struggles and her abandoning the marriage. Then he pursued! His relentless, emotional pursuit of Lucy included frequent texts, phone calls, and emails begging Lucy to not leave him and profuse apologies for all of the ways he thought he'd failed the marriage. In short, he launched a full-court press and put himself at the mercy of Lucy's response.

Let's be clear: it is noble for James to look first at himself and own his failures. In fact, doing so is always a prerequisite to confronting another about their sin (Matthew 7:1–5). However, taking responsibility for our own actions does not include enabling another down their wayward path. Remember, the wayward world is convoluted. So responding the way James did to Lucy does little to draw the prodigal to Christ—it often has the opposite effect. We need to remember that Jesus' teachings are not something we can just set aside to "make things right." The world that Jesus and his disciples lived in was just as convoluted and marred by sin as our world today, and Jesus' teachings were just as radical and counter to natural human instincts then as they sound to us today. The gospel is always foolishness to our ears, but it is the power of God to transform wayward hearts.

In our case here, knowing that James will own the blame and responsibility is quite convenient for Lucy; it empowers her to continue her wayward path. She avoids the confrontational word of God by avoiding culpability for her choices and actions. The good news that she hears is not the gospel; it is that her selfish soul can continue to pursue her sin without any consequence or fear of bad fruit.

As we discussed previously, wayward people gain power through control. Lucy now controls the joystick and will perceive James's acquiescence as weakness, which in turn gives her little incentive to change. But something important is at play here that goes beyond understanding the dynamics of a wayward mind. James has to also understand and come to trust that the word of God is true and powerful and that it can influence change in a wayward person's heart.

We often think that the word people need to hear is the unconditional acceptance that no matter what, everything will be okay. This leads us to share a gospel that lacks the power to transform. As we saw in the last chapter, the good news is not good news if it accommodates sin and fails to lead people to repentance. We want our prodigals to change, and sometimes that means they must first leave home and "come to themselves." Their change may not involve us directly.

We know this will sound paradoxical to some: *God sometimes pursues us by releasing us.* Some heart habits—ongoing, deliberate, entrenched sinful behaviors—can be dealt with only by release into the consequences. Sometimes a behavior becomes so endemic to personality that even our best counsel makes no difference. This is one of the few times where "let go, let God" is truly applicable. We release our loved one to the consequences of their choices and to the inevitable crisis that will follow. This crisis point may be God's way of forcing the wayward soul to see what life apart from God and others really looks like. It's reality therapy. God allows those he loves to experience the temporal consequences of their stupid choices in the hope of saving them from the eternal consequences of rejecting him forever.

Prodigals are often faced with a choice between two paths. The first involves destructive relationships that prodigals crave. The second is key resources that prodigals need to indulge their choices. As long as prodigals are allowed to walk the first path without having to experience the consequences of the second, they have little motivation to change because they don't experience loss and fail to see how much they truly need Christ and the gospel.

But don't take our word for it. Let's look at three biblical examples to understand what this redemptive release looks like as we begin to draw lessons and principles for engaging our own prodigals.

Creation and the Fall

Earlier, we looked at the tragedy of the sin of Adam and Eve. This first tragic drama in history was performed not in a theater, but in a garden. Adam and Eve, created to live in perfect harmony with God, were cast out of the garden of Eden over a piece of fruit.

Of course, they weren't expelled simply over pears or pineapples. It was their grab for radical autonomy, their desire to seek their own way, to forge their own course, to pursue independence from God. That's what really sent Adam and Eve packing "east of Eden."

What was truly unique about the season before human sin was that God gave humankind complete freedom and an unencumbered ability to worship him. What did we do with that freedom and ability? We traded it for slavery. In choosing to believe the lies of the serpent and exalt ourselves to be like God, men and women were born into the bondage of sin and misery from that point forward. Back in the garden days, God did not have to coerce Adam and Eve to occupy the roles for which they were created. The story was all good, even very good (Genesis 1:31). And they were free to rest in, or to reject, God's goodness.

If we take a closer look at the Fall and the consequences that followed the disobedience of Adam and Eve, we see the first outline of God's pattern of redemptive release. God could have put seraphim around the tree with forbidden fruit, ready to administer an angelic slap-down should Adam and Eve even think about straying. But he did not. Adam and Eve had the freedom to exercise their love for God and their faith in God through obedience to his Word. God did not want contrived and coerced obedience.

But this freedom carries with it consequences for disobedience. When our first parents rejected the goodness and beauty of faithfully fulfilling their God-ordained roles, their Father released them to the consequences. Instead of allowing them to live forever in a state of willful rebellion, God's consequences for Adam and Even included a dose of reality, a taste of what life without God is like. This taste would serve the redemptive purpose of awakening them to their need for God's grace as their only hope.

God cursed Adam and Eve, frustrating their attempts to fulfill the goals and the roles he had created them for. In their work, they experienced fruitless toil (Genesis 3:17–19). In their relationships, they experienced discord and a struggle for power and control (Genesis 3:16). And they would forever face the struggle of living in a world that was working against them and an enemy who wanted nothing but to steal from, destroy, and kill them. In their separation from God and his releasing them to experience the consequences of their sin, they would come to see that their only hope lay in the salvation of God's merciful intervention on their behalf.

God clothed Adam and Eve and gave them hope in the promise that he will provide an offspring who will crush their enemy's head (Genesis 3:15 NIV). But he would not allow them to enjoy his gifts without enjoying him. That would only enable their destructive selfishness. Only through release could Adam and Eve begin to fathom just how much they needed the One who loved them.

So God let them go.

The Prodigal Son

Earlier, we looked briefly at the story of the famous prodigal son who wished his father was dead and left home to squander his inheritance. Take a moment and imagine you're the father of that child. How would you have responded to his request?

While we don't know the father's motives, we can assume he saw that nothing he could say or do would change his son's mind. So he released his son to leave and experience the life he so desperately wanted. This is hard to believe, knowing the depth of the father's love that we see later in the story, but the father let him go.

Here's what didn't happen: The prodigal son didn't get to

"cash out" and then loaf around the family's estate. That arrangement would have not been acceptable. If he wanted a life separate and apart from the father's love and protection, that was what he would get. The father didn't enable him. So the son wasn't afforded the privilege of sitting around the house as an entitled man-child, having an equal share of both money and free time. He went to a distant country. He went because he *had* to go. By asking for his inheritance, he requested his complete release (physical, geographical, financial, spiritual, relational). As hard as it was, the father gave him exactly what he craved.

Recall what we said earlier about what a prodigal really wants. "Leaving without loss" is one of the most common prodigal cravings. But the father in this story denied his son that option. The younger son wanted to "leave," and the father arranged it. His response of "If you don't want to be here, I'm not going to hold you back" was probably the hardest thing he ever did. But here's the thing: What the father did in this story is also one of the most loving things he could do. Sometimes God gives us exactly what we want so the consequences teach us what we need to learn.

When we release prodigals to the fruit of their choices—instead of enabling them, controlling them, or bribing them—God's redemptive work has a chance to run its course.

As we also saw earlier, the prodigal son eventually "came to himself." Some Bible translations say that "he came to his senses"—that necessary first step in the repentance process. God sometimes shows his grace by releasing us to pursue what we want until we see what we really need—him! This is love God-style. And this love is hard to do, really hard. When we release someone, we're no longer in charge of the outcome—we relinquish any influence we have and give the person and situation to God.

The father released his son; then he waited. Not days, or weeks, probably months or more. The son had to go and live a separate life, reaping what he had sown and experiencing famine. Ultimately, his rebellion had to run its course in order for him to "come to his senses."

Sometimes sanity takes time to boomerang back home.

The Adulterous Husband

Another example of this idea of "pursuing by releasing" is found in Paul's letters to the Corinthians. In these letters, we are introduced to the Corinthian church and an uncomfortable, awkward situation. A man is in an incestuous, adulterous relationship with his father's wife (1 Corinthians 5). Paul makes it crystal clear that this sin is serious and that the church's response has actually complicated the problem. For reasons not entirely clear to us, the church chose to accommodate this sin, perpetuating and empowering this adulterous relationship. The Corinthians' stance toward this immoral situation made the entitled sinner more comfortable in his wayward behavior. He's an example of the prodigal who "has it all": the comfort, security, and safety net of a spiritual community, as well as the carnal pleasure of an illicit relationship.

So Paul teaches the Corinthian church about rugged love and redemptive release. He commands the church to discipline this man by *removing him* from fellowship; he is to be excommunicated from the church and released to experience life outside the Christian community. This is how they are to love this man. Hebrews 12:5–11 tells us that the Lord disciplines those he loves and that such discipline is a sign of his love. Paul describes the release this way: "You are to deliver this man to Satan for the destruction of the flesh, so that his spirit may be saved in the day of the Lord" (1 Corinthians 5:5). Paul's end game is clear: by experiencing temporal consequences for his sin, the man may yet be saved from eternal consequences. Though this release may seem vindictive in the short-term, it is truly an act of loving discipline designed to care for and really save the man's soul.

The process of release as church discipline *is different* from the release of a prodigal living in sin in that such discipline is directed and guided by the leadership of the church. However, both kinds of releasing *have the same purpose* and goal in mind—to separate the wayward from the life that perpetuates their destructive entitlement.

By taking the steps of removing him from fellowship, the immoral man can no longer reap the benefits of both worlds. Instead, he must experience life outside of the church and the loss of security, fellowship, friendships, and a protective leadership. According to 2 Corinthians 2, this action appears to have worked—the redemptive releasing had its intended effect. The immoral brother experienced a godly sorrow that led to repentance, a change of heart that transformed his relationship with God and with those in his local church who loved him.

The Deserting Spouse

But if the unbelieving partner separates, let it be so.

1 CORINTHIANS 7:15

Each of the previous examples is instructive for us, but let's conclude by looking at how Paul addresses a situation that more closely parallels the struggle of dealing with a wayward loved one. In 1 Corinthians 7, Paul takes up the case of a spouse who decides to leave a marriage. "Let's imagine," Paul begins, "that an unbelieving spouse wants to leave home. What should the other spouse do?" He sits silently for a minute then whispers his answer: "Let it be so."

Let it be so? No clinging, no groveling, no taking-one-for-the-team because of the kids? Paul knows they've all been tried. He also knows that the wayward spouse hasn't been manipulated out of the home; they have deserted it. So he makes it simple: "Let go." Paul sanctions the separation and frees the remaining spouse by saying, "The brother or the sister is not bound in such circumstances" (1 Corinthians 7:15 NIV).[4]

Let's not overlook the reason Paul gives for releasing the person. He gives it immediately in the same verse: "God has called you to peace." Somehow, under these trying conditions, letting go fulfills the call to peace. What does peace mean here? It may be the peace that settles on the home when the wayward spouse is gone. It may be the peace that bathes your *soul* when you exercise the courage to let go. It may be that letting go actually puts the prodigal on a path of peace and, hopefully, an appointment with the Prince of Peace. Perhaps all of these are in view here.

Sometimes to fulfill the call to peace, we must actually speak words that seal a separation—words that break our heart and detonate our dreams for what marriage should deliver right now; words no bride or groom ever dreamed they would utter. We must speak words that acknowledge that God's peace can still be found within the crimson strokes received from separation.

Let it be so.

BACK TO OUR STORY

"What should I do?" That was James's question. The answer eluded him for many weeks. His impulse to keep the peace and attempt to hold things together did not immediately bring things to a head. Lucy continued to pursue a life of independence from James, while at the same being allowed to have unfettered access to the kids, to enjoy financial security, and to have a headquarters from which she could pursue her disobedience.

But as James broadened his understanding of love, some of the themes we're discussing here began to take root. He became convinced that he could no longer continue on a path that only empowered Lucy in her sin. James insisted that Lucy join him in telling their story to their pastors and elders, asking for their prayer, help, and counsel. In addition, he brought several trusted family friends and confidants into the loop to not only ask for prayer, but also to help Lucy better understand how her choices were impacting everyone around her.

Further, James insisted that Lucy "pay her own way," that she take financial responsibility for her choices. James wanted Lucy to understand that rebellion has many costs that she must be prepared to pay. James moved forward in faith by insisting that Lucy take full responsibility for the path she had chosen for herself. His prayerful goal was to give her exactly what she wanted so the consequences would tutor her in what she really lacked.

Consequences, like change, take time. But as the weeks passed, Lucy came face-to-face with what life would really look like if she continued on her self-declared journey of indulgence and disobedience. No more financial safety net, no more relationships without responsibility, no more home, and no more security. As she carefully counted the cost, Lucy joined the prodigal son in "coming to her senses."

As a result, Lucy turned toward James, slowly but decidedly. Their time apart gave her space to truly think about the implications of her decisions. An alien question appeared: *Do I really want to squander all the blessings that have come with twenty years of marriage?* In a moment of unexpected honesty, Lucy realized she just couldn't give it all up.

If this were a romance novel, we would see a climactic confession and immediate resolution. But reconciliation in a sinful world moves more slowly. Yes, Lucy did come to a point where she sincerely repented before God. But James and Lucy still had plenty of debris to identify and clear from their path. Their church and church elders there joined them for the journey by surrounding them with love, care, and counsel. God was faithful, and slowly they rebuilt their marriage. That was more than twenty years ago.

When James and Lucy tell their story today, people are stunned. They can't imagine that a marriage that is now so solid and enduring could have been so perilously close to ending. But divorce seemed inevitable until James set free what he loved and trusted God with what he could not control. James exercised faith. And Lucy found God.

Of course, not every story will end this way. For every miracle like Lucy and James's, there are marriages that end in separation and are never reconciled. Redemptive release is not a magic formula that fixes every problem. But it is a step we need to take if we are to have *any* hope of healing.

Trust God with your prodigal. He has a way with those who stray. Your job right now is to love them courageously, even if that means letting them go. It's God's job to bring them home.

How Do We Know When It's Time to Let Go?

I f you love someone, set them free. If they come back they're yours; if they don't they never were." Welcome to the seventies, where quotes like this by Richard Bach captured the masses with an illusion of insight. If you're part of the generation who wore bell-bottoms and line danced to disco as I (Dave) was, you know that discernment wasn't a generational strength. Still, Bach had one thing right. Sometimes loving someone means letting them go without knowing if they will ever come back.

If you're walking with someone who is going down the wayward road, you may be experiencing a growing realization that letting go is the next step. In fact, you might have reached this conclusion several chapters ago. Yet letting go may feel less like a step and more like a flying leap off a 500-foot cliff. You want to be sure. You *need* to be sure.

How do you know when to let go? And is there any guarantee that it will work?

KNOWING WHEN IT'S TIME

The following questions will not give you a detailed road map for your own situation. We wish we could offer that, but since every relationship is unique, there is no formula to follow. What we can offer are markers or guideposts to help you plot a course forward.

Think of them as road signs—indicators that signal when it's time to start looking at the route of redemptive release.

Have You Prayed Fervently?

Yes, we talked about prayer earlier. But some things are so important, they bear repeating. This is one. Paul tells the Thessalonians to "pray without ceasing" (1 Thessalonians 5:17). We say you need to pray not because prayer is one of those mandatory points that must be added to every checklist. We say it because prayer is essential to the type of battle we are engaged in. Rebellious waywardness is a spiritual battle, and we're not wrestling against flesh and blood (Ephesians 6:12). You can't fight with words and reasonable arguments alone. In fact, Scripture provides piercing insight on what lies behind a prodigal's flight, and it's pretty diabolical. "In their case the god of this world has blinded the minds of the unbelievers, to keep them from seeing the light of the gospel of the glory of Christ, who is the image of God" (2 Corinthians 4:4).

Pray—because Satan has struck someone you love with mental blindness. Two couples we know who each have wayward teens decided to make a conference call each day to pray together. They committed to thirty days. During the call, they took one minute to greet each other and then cried out to God for the next fourteen minutes. They asked God to intervene and wage war on behalf of their kids.

Be ready for things to change in unexpected ways when you pray. Things will often get *worse* before they get better. For both sets of parents, their kid's rebellion worsened, and they had to let them go. But within a few weeks of leaving home, God began to move in powerful ways to humble their children and draw them back to himself. A year later, the fruit of those prayers is undeniable. If you ask these parents why their children changed, they'll point to that time of prayer.

Remember: only God is big enough to win this battle. To engage him for our cause, we must pray.

But there's another reason to pray. If you're reading this book, you undoubtedly feel spent. Spiritually exhausted. You've already left it all out on the field only to realize the game has just started. Yes, your prodigal needs prayer. But you need it too! You need strength; you need help; you need power. You need to be filled with the Holy Spirit (Romans 15:13).

So pray. Steadily, constantly, unswervingly . . . pray! (Ephesians 6:18). God is your ever-present help in trouble (Psalm 46:1), and he wants to hear what you need.

Does This Person Have Psychological Problems?

At times sinful and foolish behavior is being fueled by unrecognized physical or psychological problems, issues that make normal interventions largely ineffective. In extreme cases, clinical factors can be at play that may be diminishing the prodigal's capacity to accurately judge right from wrong. A bi-polar spouse needs to be properly evaluated and may need medication. When patterns of irrational or harmful behavior arise, it's wise to immediately involve outside experts who are trained to address these kinds of issues. We say this not to replace pastoral care and counseling but to supplement it. Our brokenness manifests in many forms, some physical, others spiritual, and a holistic response is required to address the problems we face.

For example, Kate in our second chapter would be very wise to consult a trusted counselor and physician who could engage and examine her son. Getting help like this should not be done with the goal of excusing bad behavior. Rather, it's incumbent upon someone like Blake's mom to find out if other extenuating factors are at play, such as depression, suicidal thoughts, posttraumatic stress, or chemical dependency. If so, those issues will need to be addressed. Kate cannot ignore the rebellion that underlies Blake's choices, but medication, testing, ongoing counseling, or even hospitalization might also be called for.

One of the great difficulties in navigating this issue is that we live in a world where a therapeutic interpretation of human behavior is pervasive—to the exclusion of biblical understanding of how people's motives and actions are shaped and expressed. Almost anyone who visits a mental health professional can walk away with some sort of clinical diagnosis attached to his or her behavior. While this diagnosis can be helpful, it will not address the entire person.

Clinical, therapeutic solutions rarely address the spiritual issues at stake. This is why prodigal sufferers need to consult with their pastor, other Christians in their church, and Christian counselors and psychologists. Doing so will help ensure they're getting trusted, biblical counsel about the best way to proceed, and that the diagnostic process doesn't abandon Scripture. These engagements will enable families to properly weight the physiological contribution as they evaluate whether it's time to let go.

Have Your Words Lost All Influence?

Words form the fabric that clothes our human relationships. Words also reveal the condition of the human heart (Luke 6:45). To understand whether our words can carry any redemptive influence, two essential questions must be answered.

First, *are they habitually lying?* While lying often unleashes havoc on a relationship (Proverbs 26:28; Isaiah 32:7) , it isn't

always a mark of someone in a state of unrestrained waywardness. All people are susceptible to hiding their sin and lying to
cover up. But prodigals display a habitual pattern of deception.
As the consequences pile up, personal responsibility slips away,
and the narrative of "me as victim" takes over. The weaknesses
or sins of parents, spouse, and loved ones become the real reason
for their woes. This aggrieved status, when mingled with self-
pity over the consequences of their choices, exonerates prodigals
from any sense they may have of personal responsibility.

It's hard for prodigals to speak truth when they're working so
hard to deny it.

Sadly, it's not uncommon for some people within your relational network to listen sympathetically to the wayward person's
twisted worldview and even take up their offense. Try to be understanding, as it can be difficult for those who are not involved with
the person on a daily basis to accurately see the truth. We've heard
stories of people opening their homes to other people's rebellious
kids after hearing one-sided reports of harsh treatment from
their parents. Soon they discover the truth. One of the take-
homes here is that leaders, other parents, and the church should
be particularly vigilant, ready to listen to all parties involved and
prayerfully doing their best to discern the truth. A person fleeing
from God's truth is typically a poor witness to it.

If you love someone who is straying, pay attention to communication patterns. Chronic, habitual deceit not only erodes the
relational foundation of trust but also signals that your present
strategy is not working. Serial lying probably means it's time to
pivot.

Second, *is the person listening to you?* You may have heard the
playground taunt, "I'm rubber, and you're glue; whatever you say

bounces off me and sticks to you!" When dealing with a prodigal, your words are subject to the law of diminishing returns.
Prodigals become so hardened to input and correction that their
hearts are more like a piece of Teflon than a sponge. You'll quickly
recognize when your words are being deflected, not absorbed. If
this is happening, it's a sign that to the wayward person, you've
become part of the problem, not part of the solution.

If your words are being deflected and the wayward person
believes you are part of the problem, then your words have lost all
influence, and you need to forge a new direction.

Have You Suffered Long with Little Fruit?

As we saw in chapter 6, our patience and longsuffering are
important means God uses to expose and crush folly in the
heart of a fool. These spiritual fruits are like holy antiseptic on
a soul's wound, working constantly beneath the surface to bring
healing. Yet at times our longsuffering patience is met with an
equally stubborn resistance. When this happens, a boundless
forbearance can serve to accommodate sin rather than serving
the sinner. An environmental change may be needed.

Blake's mom is an example. For years, she placed the accent
on patience as she wrestled with him over his wayward indulgences. She did not want to respond disproportionately in anger
and exasperation toward him. After all, it is the kindness of the
Lord that leads to repentance (Romans 2:4). However, over time,
Kate began to see that her kindness *wasn't* leading to Blake's
repentance; it was only adding weight to the two-ton mound of
folly he was dumping on the family.

God's patience carries the power to achieve God's will. Ours
does not.

Remember: the wayward are prone to take advantage of human patience. This tendency does not excuse us from showing patience—we must be willing to love our prodigal by embodying the gospel for an extended season. But a truly prodigal heart exploits longsuffering by treating it as an open invitation to unaccountable indulgence. In this case, it may be time to convert the safe passage they enjoy at home into a temporary visa to another place.

Agreements and Commitments?

To live in a home is to live under house rules. Every family has their own commitments and agreements that keep the peace and hold the family together. These can be as simple and mundane as completing chores and household tasks, or as weighty as being faithful to marital vows and sexual standards. When you are living with a prodigal, though, commitments become ammunition in the fight for freedom.

When Blake could not be trusted to abide by his curfew, Kate was left with a problem that no amount of his apologies could fix. His broken curfew represented several deeper issues—habitual lies, drug abuse, sexual promiscuity. It meant that Blake was now living life entirely on his own terms. His problems were threatening the very fabric of family life.

It's the challenge of managing the prodigal's environment that brings the choice to let go into sharper relief. Each family's capacity to absorb the body blows of wayward behavior will be different. However, some threshold markers might be helpful in making the decision to let a loved one suffer the consequences of their choices:

- Is this person endangering himself or others?
- Is he or she unwilling to make promises/commitments or acknowledge when they have failed to keep them? In commenting on adult prodigals, Jim Newheiser and Elyse Fitzpatrick have written: "Wayward adult children often lie to avoid consequences or to get what they want from others. Honesty should be a nonnegotiable condition of turning your home into a halfway house. If a pattern of dishonesty continues, the privilege of living at home must be forfeited."[5]
- Have those responsible for or married to this person lost the capacity to curtail or contain their comings and goings?
- Are illegal, immoral, or dangerous elements being introduced into the home such as drugs, guns, alcohol, gambling, or illicit sexual activity?

While this list is far from exhaustive, a "yes" to one of these four questions reveals that you've lost the ability to engage, speak into, and influence a prodigal. Letting go in the present may be the only way to secure their future.

APPLYING THE QUESTIONS—A STORY OF HOPE

This was not Ashley's first visit to her pastor's office, but it would be her most important. She and Matt, her husband, had been meeting with their pastor off and on for over a year. Matt had a history of abusing alcohol and going to disturbing lengths to conceal it from Ashley. Matt's behavior had not only drained the trust account in their marriage; it had rendered him unable to hold a steady job and provide financially for his family. Ashley and her son, Tommy, hung suspended by a thread over a pit of emotional and economic disaster.

With the help of her pastor, Ashley began to understand the basics of rugged love: Matt was confronted, Ashley's pain was given a voice, and consequences were enforced. All of this happened while Ashley served Matt with patience, kindness, and a forgiving spirit. For the next few months, it all appeared to be working. But sadly, this appearance was an illusion. Shortly thereafter, Ashley learned that Matt had been deceiving her. And his web of duplicity was staggering.

First, she stumbled upon a stash of hard liquor in Matt's car trunk. As Ashley slammed the trunk shut, a stray thought chilled her to the bone: this was only the iceberg's tip. She ran in the house to find the hidden pile of credit card receipts. A few minutes of further searching led her to a secret account that Matt was using to fund his addictive behavior. Ashley blinked back the tears as she accessed his Visa card and saw the astronomical balance accruing interest with the passing of every day. The final blow came when she realized that Matt was missing work and consequently missing paychecks.

The family was in a full-blown financial, relational, and spiritual crisis.

Ashley sat slumped in a chair at her pastor's office, wrestling with the same question we have been grappling with here: *Was it time to let Matt go?* It was all too evident that her words had little impact on her husband. Matt had become a master manipulator and a chronic liar. Ashley couldn't trust a word he said. There seemed to be little lasting fruit from her months and months of longsuffering. In addition, Matt wouldn't keep any agreements. And now it appeared his bondage to alcohol required additional resources they didn't have. Ashley was overwhelmed. She needed time, and she now realized that Matt needed a different kind of help. Help she could not provide to him.

It was time to let Matt go.

Under her pastor's care, Ashley took Tommy and moved across the country to live with her parents. She worked out specific guidelines required for reconciliation with Matt, including securing qualified help for his alcoholism. She also insisted that he secure a permanent job and support his family. Equally important to her was that Matt meet regularly with the leadership of his church for support and accountability.

Ashley chose rugged love. By the grace of God, Matt began the slow, excruciating turn away from his sins and back toward Jesus. It wasn't easy—he worked long and fought temptation morning, noon, and night. Matt hated to be alone but began to see his situation as a consequence of his own choices. He wept; he worked. Over time, repentance bore fruit, and new convictions found fertile ground in Matt's heart.

Twelve months later, Ashley and Tommy returned to live with Matt. Matt was still a sinner, but now he had taken steps to repent and love his family. That was three years ago, and Matt and Ashley are doing much better, always aware of their need for God's help each day.

A rugged love emboldened Ashley to let go. And rugged love won.

AS THEY GO

Because we all live in the real world, we know these situations sometimes roll differently. Letting go is not some kind of magic dust sprinkled on sinners that instantly opens their eyes. Only grace gives sight. Just like the wayward son in the prodigal story, there may be a great gulf between their departure as an unrepentant and unreconciled fool and their return to their senses (Luke 15:17).

Note the word "unreconciled." When you love a prodigal, the painful reality is that you feel unreconciled to them. Most often there's no send-off, no goodbye kisses—just hard words, slammed doors, and empty threats. With the prodigal goes a piece of your heart that you hope will be returned one day. And what remains is the memories of their biting retorts and loveless actions that have shredded the relational fiber connecting you to them.

So what do we do as we watch our prodigal go and settle in for the wait? Or what do we do if they're already gone, and it seems like our prodigal just won't repent?

Forgive Persistently

Here's a radical thought. You don't need your prodigal's apology or repentance to begin the process of forgiving. A prodigal sufferer can exercise the muscle of forgiveness regardless of where their prodigal lands. "For if you forgive others their trespasses, your heavenly Father will also forgive you" (Matthew 6:14). This of course does not mean the two of you are reconciled, but you prepare your heart to forgive by ridding your heart of bitterness and applying the gospel in preparation for their return (Ephesians 4:31).

In his outstanding book *Come Back, Barbara*, written about his daughter's waywardness, Jack Miller says,

> Forgiveness . . . has stages. At first you forgive the person who
> has not changed and persists in evil behavior. You forgive in

the hope that in time the person will repent. Next, you deepen your forgiveness when the person expresses repentance and shows the fruit of a changed life. At this stage you welcome the repentant person fully into your fellowship.[6]

The hard part of living in stage one of forgiveness is, of course, the relational limitations with the unrepentant prodigal. True reconciliation cannot take place apart from repentance, which means some relational guardrails must be erected until the offending party genuinely repents. It isn't wise or healthy to give unfettered entrée into our hearts and lives to someone who repeatedly, serially, and grievously sins against us.

Consider the example of a man whose wife refuses to be faithful to him. Is there an expectation or requirement in Scripture that they continue to relate to one another as if this sort of relational treachery was not taking place? The answer, of course, is "no" (Matthew 18:15–18; 1 Corinthians 5:9–11). In fact, this kind of sin must be addressed boldly and ruggedly, with relational standing wisely recalibrated. Yet even in the worst situations, forgiveness and reconciliation are never farther away than personal repentance (2 Corinthians 2:5–11).

However, if you love a prodigal in this fallen world, you have no guarantee that you will be reconciled with them. Not all relational ills are resolved in this life. Persistent forgiveness pleases God, not because it purchases your prodigal's repentance, but because it reflects the Savior's work (Colossians 3:13).

Suffer in Community

Loving the wayward is a form of suffering. Suffering tends to isolate us. This means that loving the wayward can be a lonely path.

Don't let it be.

To be in a relationship with a prodigal is akin to living in captivity. Feelings of shame, anger, guilt, and fear scrape you raw and make it difficult for you to think clearly. You need to rely on the wisdom and counsel of pastors and church communities in moving forward.

This support becomes particularly necessary as your prodigal walks toward the light of repentance. It's very hard for a person who has been repeatedly sinned against to measure the sincerity of the sinner's repentance. Without the help of wise friends or trusted leaders, we can define repentance arbitrarily through our feelings rather than through the prodigal's words and actions. Our experience makes us vulnerable to holding past sins over the head of prodigals who desire to repent. We smuggle in bitterness and anger toward a prodigal because they don't seem quite contrite enough for our taste.

These feelings are why we should never assign ourselves the "sinned against" status without the wisdom and perspective of outside help. We must avoid the "tyranny of the aggrieved," when those sinned against withhold forgiveness and reconciliation until the sinner meets all of their expectations or demands. Church leaders and pastors can help prodigal sufferers measure the sincerity and substance of repentance. God gives us leaders and a faith community in the church to help us navigate these gut-wrenching decisions so that our faucet of forgiveness can flow freely and wisely.

Helping to evaluate repentance is not the only maze the church helps us navigate. Prodigals who are believers are often church members too. In this case, their waywardness is an invitation by God's Spirit through God's Word to engage God's leaders to apply God's discipline. Passages like Matthew 18:15–20 and 1 Corinthians 5:1–13 arm leaders to serve wayward Christians with rugged love expressed through biblical discipline.

The church participated in Ashley's story. At the lowest and most terrifying moment of her life, she resisted the impulse to isolate herself and pressed into her local church. Doing so ensured that Matt experienced the unique grace that comes from and to those who live under local church authority. Through the wise advice and determined love of their pastor, Matt began to respond. Loving discipline—the kind that flows from spiritual people with gentle hearts (Galatians 6:1)—wooed the sinner back to the Savior. Looking back, Matt says the rugged love of his church was a key feature in his turn back to God and his family.

LET THE GOLDEN RULE GUIDE YOU

Not every story ends like Matt and Ashley's. Or if it does, it takes months or even years before prodigals repent and turn back to the Lord or to the people they have wronged. You may have few interactions and little margin for error when you talk. So how do you keep the train of progress on the track instead of careening off the cliff?

Enter the Golden Rule. The Golden Rule is just a pithy way of saying Luke 6:31, "And as you wish that others would do to you, do so to them." This means treating prodigals the way you would want to be treated if you were in their shoes. By doing so, you are communicating that prodigals are people made in God's image with the ability to choose their own course in life. Certainly, they have distorted this image through their destructive choices. Yet their personhood as an individual created in the image of God and the love you've experienced through the gospel should provide the foundation for your ongoing interaction.

Interacting by the Golden Rule means you are accepting, but not embracing, their new identity. A gay son? Let him know his lifestyle doesn't change your heart for him. He is still your son, and you love him. A delinquent daughter? Sure, you have concerns, but your love for her is unchanged. An adulterous spouse? Same thing. You grieve the sin but love the sinner. Let your spouse know you're no longer going to try to control their behavior. Make sure he or she knows that you see controlling others as wrong, and you wouldn't want anyone doing it to you.

Again, turn to the Golden Rule. Isn't it how *you* would want others to treat you if the roles were reversed?

Love, even when we show it to difficult people, is never passive. Remain on the lookout for ways to serve and do good to this person, even if he or she considers you to be "the enemy." Recall what we said earlier about overcoming evil with good. A prodigal can still be surprised and shocked into spiritual sobriety by unexpected acts of kindness.

One of the things Ashley did for Matt during their period of separation was to arrange for him to fly across the country to visit her and Tommy. They spent the weekend together talking through relational issues and giving Matt opportunities to reconnect with his son. In extending this kindness to Matt, Ashley was not capitulating on their agreement. Rather, she was looking for meaningful ways to touch his heart even while she waited for his full repentance. As a result, Matt knew that Ashley was still "for" him, even as she demonstrated rugged love toward him. Her actions served to draw him back toward his marriage, his promises to her, and his God.

LOOKING AHEAD: LETTING GO IS HARD TO DO

As you read this chapter, you may be experiencing faint hope as you realize you can do more before you consider letting go. Perhaps reading this chapter has confirmed in your heart that now is not the time and more needs to be done before you reach this place in your relationship.

Or you may be facing one of the saddest moments of your life. You have come to believe that letting go is your next step, and you're fighting back your fears. Here's what you need you to know: fear is your greatest temptation and your biggest adversary.

Ultimately, letting go is not about trusting yourself or the person who has hurt you—it's about trusting Jesus. Right now it may seem like this person is your project, and the only acceptable outcome is for them to change and for life to return to "normal." But you are beginning to see that a bigger plan is at work here— one so magnificent that it includes God's love and care for you! You're about to experience his presence and comfort in ways you never dreamed possible. Your wayward spouse, friend, or child may be the problem, but your transformation is also part of God's greater plan.

Don't be afraid. Trust Jesus. He will surprise you.

PART THREE

Rugged Grace

CHAPTER 9

The Shame of Loving the Wayward

There is something those who love the wayward refer to as "the walk of shame." We're not talking about the "morning-after" stagger from where you just spent the night, or the silent shuffle alongside the security guard after you cleared out your desk because of job cuts. Another sort of shame is common to the struggles we're talking about in this book. It greets you each morning and scrubs you raw by the end of the day. It's the shame of being paired with a prodigal. Your life and identity are wrapped up in your connection to a straying spouse, a truant sibling, a wayward child. Someone you love has screwed everything up, and they've left you to explain and sometimes even to defend what they have done.

We understand.

THE SHAME DISPENSER

Being paired with a prodigal is a relational nightmare. Imagine a person who, due to idolatry, addiction, or brain chemistry, lives as if there are no rules—only rights. *Their* rights! Add a strong dose of violation, butter it with entitlement, and pepper it with victimhood. What happens? You get a human hurricane on a collision course with personal self-destruction and familial devastation. The home becomes a federal disaster area pretty quickly.

But that's just the beginning.

Take that prodigal and assassinate his conscience so that moral reasoning and personal responsibility are excised. But give him a voice—one that thunders about injustice or seethes with silent hostility. He regularly feels violated by crimes undetected by others, but according to him are deserving of capital punishment. Then plant him smack dab in the middle of a marriage or a family, and the entire group's happiness will be dependent upon how he is doing at any given hour. He's a full frontal "identity assault" on the family, one that tears the heart in two and tars the soul with humiliation.

Added to this is the burden of how others see you. Wayward souls rarely have a muffler. They curse, vomit, demand, scream, and cry. They acquaint you with indignities. Their sin may be private, but their flight from God easily becomes public fodder. The behavior of someone you love incites the chatter of others.

To love a prodigal is to live exposed.

This means the sense of condemnation you feel is not just inward but outward. The shame affixed to your soul is not just what you feel about yourself but can come from what others say or how they treat you.

UNDER SUSPICION

The most damaging element is the suspicion. Veiled inferences within your social network send a clear message that some people, perhaps many, trace a straight line between your faults and your prodigal's choices. It's bad fruit, they say—the jury coming in, the rooster coming home to roost, the reaping of what's been sown. In your better moments, you remain silent, wishing to God your life was as simple as their logic.

More shame.

Cara knows shame. When she married John just out of college, he seemed grounded in his faith and determined in his work—a man on a mission. A few years into their marriage, financial trouble hit them like a freight train. John unraveled, became an angry man, and blamed God. Now John is emotionally withdrawn and gone for large blocks of time. Cara knows not to bring up church, or the kids, or sex, or where he goes—they're all hot-button issues. John may leave, or he may stay. Oh, and he blames Cara too.

Christians around town look at Cara with sympathy, or maybe pity; it's so hard to tell. Some wag their heads in quiet certainty, knowing that the fruit has finally spoken. They don't see how or why, but they just know the dots between John's irrationality and Cara's behavior connect in some mysterious fashion. So every morning, Cara wakes and thinks to herself: I don't get it. If he's the one AWOL from God and his family, why do I feel the shame?

When we're yoked with the shameful, we often wear the shame they deny.

Cara feels exposed, inferior, and rejected. And it doesn't take long for those *feelings* to become what she believes about herself. What do we say to Cara? How can God help her? Or let's make it more personal: How can God help you?

GOOD NEWS FOR THE SHAMED

Therefore, since we are surrounded by so great a cloud of witnesses, let us also lay aside every weight, and sin which clings so closely, and let us run with endurance the race that is set before us, looking to Jesus, the founder and perfecter of our faith, who for the joy that was set before him endured the cross, despising the shame, and is seated at the right hand of the throne of God.

> Consider him who endured from sinners such hostility against himself, so that you may not grow weary or fainthearted.
>
> *HEBREWS 12:1–3*

The writer of Hebrews reminds us that a great cloud of witnesses is amassed in heaven. Before you respond in fear to the idea of others watching you, know that they're a crowd of friends. They gather not for a public trial but to remind us there's happiness beyond heartbreak, that this life isn't our hope and isn't the end. And they know of what they speak! This crowd is filled with those who lost loved ones, had families that failed, are saints who sinned, and are God-lovers who died with broken dreams (Hebrews 11:39).

They are people who know shame.

They are gathered to testify of God's power in our pain, to remind us that the calamities we endure are worth it, and to shout that shame isn't the final word. Hebrews 11 also tells stories of God-lovers who, by the world's standards, were successes. They defeated great armies and saw their loved ones revived. But these aren't perfect people either. They weren't spared from trials or struggles. They were imperfect God-lovers who, like their counterparts who experienced unspeakable heartbreak, had one thing in common—their unbridled devotion to God. The writer of Hebrews offers us the key that is able to set people like Cara free—people who are imprisoned behind the bars of disgrace.

FREEDOM STARTS BY LAYING ASIDE SHAME

The author of Hebrews reminds us that regardless of their earthly highs and lows, the stories of these witnesses ended well; in fact they're now happy and whole in heaven. They made it, and now make an appearance to cheer us on. The writer says, *"Since we are surrounded by so great a cloud of witnesses, let us also lay aside every weight, and sin which clings so closely"* (Hebrews 12:1).

As the witnesses watch, we're told to lay aside "every weight." Since the writer mentions sin next, it's evident that these weights are something distinct from sin. So "laying aside every weight" is clearly not Bible-speak for avoiding sin; it must be something else. Something not sinful, but serious enough to hinder our progress. Such weights are the things that slow us down—burdens we lug around that make progress more difficult.

During my (Paul) more athletic teenage years, we would sometimes run wearing weighted vests. They made running—something I was never good at—more strenuous and exhausting, meaning they made me an even worse runner. The weight vest impeded my ability to move forward. It weighed me down and exhausted me.

Shame is a weight vest. Some slide it on each morning to begin the toilsome task of trudging through the day. The moment we begin to experience freedom, the words or actions of our prodigal intrude. We look down, and the weight vest suddenly appears again, dragging our soul to the ground. Life becomes about survival, not progress.

Prodigals hang a two-sided weight vest on those who love them. To shed it, we must understand both sides.

SIDE 1: HOW WE SEE OURSELVES

Shame is rude. By this we mean it is always talking—loudly, intrusively, repetitively, unforgivingly. Shame accuses. It lays blame. Your prodigal is *your* fault. Your kids' mistakes mirror your own failures. Your spouse has withdrawn because of *you*. You didn't let go; you gave up!

Of course, we're never guiltless. Therein lies the danger. A wayward person incites sin in others like Mardi Gras has come to town. There may even be ways your sins have contributed to their rebellion (see Adam and Cain). Thank God for the gospel, his reminder that our failures are never big enough to interrupt his plan for our prodigal.

Shame preaches an anti-gospel. It tells us we're inferior, or inadequate, or dishonored, or disgusting. Other people have such normal families, but not us. That's why we're unclean, or repulsive, or worthless, or filthy—and hopeless. Ed Welch says, "The language of shame is extreme. Hear it enough and you believe it. You are told you are disgusting and unclean, and eventually you *believe* you are. For many men and women who experience shame, name-calling (from others) would be redundant. They already have been calling themselves those names for years."[7]

SIDE 2: HOW OTHERS SEE US

We said it earlier: *To love a prodigal is to live exposed.* We are forced to endure the shame of all who know us, both in real life *and* online. People know about our "situation," and that's shameful. Sometimes they speak about it, which can add to the shame. Sometimes they pontificate about it, which can tempt us to find some biblical justification for slapping them upside the head.

Prodigals are clueless. Our church or community is not. Cue the shame.

One of the delicate realities of life is how well-meaning people, even decent Christian folk, can pile on when a prodigal goes public with their sin. We're not talking about ignoring honest evaluation or curbing biblical discipline for unrepentant sin. We're talking about how easily Christians can confuse redemptive discipline with dishing shame. When sin surfaces, other Christians often pile on. We become tone-deaf to each other's pain. Fortunately, God's grace is more powerful than others' self-righteousness. Carol Barnier, a popular conference speaker, discovered this weight of shame in an unexpected and surprising way the first time she was asked to tell her story publicly of dealing with her own foolish, wayward choices:

> People began coming into the room, not in a rush or with purposefulness, but rather dribbling in slowly, quietly. They took their seats far from one another, not wanting even the slightest possibility of chitchat with other attendees. A few caught me at the door and felt the need to nervously say, "I'm here for a friend, not myself."
>
> I didn't recognize it immediately, but I eventually came to know the prevailing emotion that was evident that day—shame.
>
> In retrospect, I shouldn't have been surprised. I, myself, had waited years to begin telling my own story for the same reason. I'm not proud of the path I took or the self-destructive decisions that I made. I regret the stress that I brought into my parents' home. But my reasons for keeping quiet were much more self-serving. I knew that a very real loss of status could result by sharing.[8]

The people in Carol's story didn't want to talk openly about their struggles. Everyone was afraid because of their shame. Shame is a weight borne by both the wayward and those who love them.

BREAKING FREE: TALKING TO YOURSELF

D. Martyn Lloyd Jones once asked, "Have you realized that most of your unhappiness in life is due to the fact that you're listening to yourself instead of talking to yourself?"[9] Laying aside the weight of how we see ourselves and how others see us begins with the way we talk—specifically how we speak to our own soul. Lies must encounter truth. Turmoil must hear words of peace. Condemnation must listen to the gospel. But all of this starts with talking to yourself.

Let's break it down a little more. When shame comes knocking, ask yourself, "Where is my mind?" In other words, we must look beyond our *feelings* of shame to the *ideas* that foment the feelings. What we often discover is some lingering statement, some idle fear, some subtle lie, some negative idea has taken root and is now cultivating the feeling of shame.

Remember, shame assaults identity. It tries to speak about who you are as a person. "You are a failure," it screams. "You are a terrible parent. You have totally failed as a spouse. You are a colossal mess-up, hurting everyone who comes in contact with you." Shame grows as you listen to the accusations that come from your prodigal, your community, and even yourself.

But shame begins to lose its power when you expose it to the bright rays of the gospel. The gospel overrules shame. It speaks words of reality, promise, and hope—words that arm us against the blistering accusations of shame.

Earlier, we talked about the power of the stories we believe. Shame can form the narrative of the story you tell yourself. It's a tale where you are a complete failure. You need to replace that story with the True Story, the gospel. The gospel tells you that you are a child of God. The story of shame says that your sins are too great; the gospel says that all your sins have been washed away by the blood of Christ. Shame says that you stink as a spouse or parent; the gospel says you are sin-heavy and mistake-prone, but with Jesus you always have a second chance. Shame says there's no hope for you; the gospel says that because you're in Christ, God has made extraordinary promises about your future.

Shame wants to rewrite your story. It wants to redefine your identity and give you a little paper nametag. The gospel speaks the truth about who you are, permanently branding you with Christ's perfect name. You can begin to lay aside the false narratives you speak to yourself by understanding what God thinks about you, which we learn in the gospel. The gospel reveals a love so great that God sent his Son to rescue us from our sinful corruption. What could be more true, honorable, or commendable than preaching the gospel to yourself, and doing it loud enough to silence the song of shame?

Shame runs deep. It fits the circumstances around us and describes the relational destruction we see. But we need to ask: "Is it true?" The gospel speaks at a deeper level than our shame. It tells us that we are far worse than even our shame suggests, but that we are far more loved than we can ever understand. The only way to dry up the roots of shame is by constantly and consistently unearthing these roots and exposing them to the light of the gospel.

Once you identify the roots of your shame, you need to do the work of swapping it out for your new identity in Christ. Expel your fear with a superior thought about God and his goodness. The mind truly is a remarkable organ. But it can only entertain one thought at a time. So we must swap the thought; we must export shame and import something better.

Finally, brothers, whatever is true, whatever is honorable, whatever is just, whatever is pure, whatever is lovely, whatever is commendable, if there is any excellence, if there is anything worthy of praise, think about these things.

PHILIPPIANS 4:8

Memorize this verse. Remember that shame's path is paved with specific thoughts. So each time an accusing idea begins, replace it with whatever is true, honorable, just, pure, lovely, and commendable.

But there's more. Don't just think of randomly praiseworthy things like sunsets, Handel's *Messiah*, an honest mechanic, or the last ten minutes of *A Few Good Men*. Start with the essence and apex of all that is true, honorable, pure, and commendable: the gospel itself. Consider how all of these qualities are embodied in Jesus and his finished work.

Remember, the call to "think about these things" is just another way to heed the counsel of the author of Hebrews: "consider Jesus" (Hebrews 3:1–3)!

FREEDOM FINISHES BY LOOKING TO JESUS

Shame distorts our view of God. It moves our worst moments to the middle of our field of vision. It blurs our ideas of who Jesus is and what he's done for us. Shame smears the lens through which our soul sees God.

As we write this, the Hubble telescope has just celebrated twenty-five years of being in space. Shortly after launch in 1990, NASA discovered that the main mirror was incorrectly shaped, which caused the images Hubble was sending to be distorted. So in 1993, NASA launched some Hubble optometrists with giant contact lenses that would correct the vision problem. The pictures Hubble has sent since that time redefine the word *magnificent*. Just google "Hubble," and you'll see what we mean.

The Hubble telescope reveals that space is far larger and more glorious than we ever dared to imagine. But until 1993, everything we saw from the telescope was out of focus. Once the repairs were made, we have seen the grandeur, beauty, and expanse of our small corner of space in much sharper focus and far clearer detail. And the view is exquisite!

The audience of the book of Hebrews was likely weary, fearful, and tired of the indignities suffered as an oppressed minority. Like looking through the pre-1993 Hubble, the greatness and goodness of something magnificent—God!—was obscured. As a result, it was hard for them to anticipate the future because what little they saw looked pretty hopeless. Perhaps you can relate right now.

The writer of Hebrews understands. He knows that freedom from shame comes from a sharper focus on the right things. So he tells us to look to Jesus in two distinct ways.

WHO JESUS IS

First, focus on who Jesus is. Who he *really* is. Jesus is not merely an indomitable leader, an omnicompetent counselor, or a prodigious problem-solver. He is, according to Hebrews 12:2, "the founder and perfecter of our faith." Unusual descriptors, to be sure. Let's allow these words to sharpen our vision of Jesus.

Founder of our faith is not some ceremonial title. It's linked to Hebrews 2:10 where Jesus is referred to as "the founder of [our] salvation." In view here is certainly the idea of Jesus as founder or "pioneer"—the forerunner, or preeminent example of complete confidence in God.

Yet this phrase also means that Jesus is the author, the originator, the source, and the instigator of our faith. Our saving trust in God is alive because Jesus created it; he literally brought it to life. Christ wasn't a cosmic midwife who helped give birth to a latent faith within us. He invented our faith from nothing. He was there in the beginning, before the foundations of the world were laid (Ephesians 1:3–6). Thus he is crowned Founder.

But Jesus doesn't just create our faith, wish us well, and wave goodbye. He's also the *Perfecter* of our faith. This means Jesus hangs around and completes what he has begun, makes sure our faith lasts, and brings it to the intended goal. This talk of perfecting work reminds us of Philippians 1:6: "And I am sure of this, that he who began a good work in you will bring it to completion at the day of Jesus Christ."

Ponder this verse for a minute. Today's shame isn't the final word. Christ is dedicated to helping you finish the race.

Shame grows when we look in the wrong direction. Imagine trying to see the moon by staring hard at the grass in your yard. It's hard to suffocate shame when our eyes are looking in the wrong place. One of our daughters used to run with her head down, not up, looking where she was going. After a few bumps and bruises, she learned a valuable lesson. The best way to run forward is by looking up.

To flee shame, we must look up at who Jesus really is. We must gaze vigilantly and unwaveringly at his commitment to help us change. Looking up brings clarity, and seeing Christ clearly speeds our release from the shackles of shame.

WHAT JESUS HAS DONE

Next, focus on what Jesus has done. Here again the writer of Hebrews helps us, "looking to Jesus . . . who for the joy that was set before him endured the cross, despising the shame, and is seated at the right hand of the throne of God" (Hebrews 12:2). This passage juxtaposes the contradictory states of joy and shame. The author of Hebrews seems to say that we should focus on the One who focused on joy. In fact, Christ's quest for joy was so empowering that it enabled him to endure death on the cross and despise the shame of it. Is it possible that our shame could be vanquished by the same quest?

"Enduring the cross" transports us back to the most shameful moment in human history. It was the dark day at Golgotha when God himself in the person of Christ was executed, hanging naked while he bore a torturous punishment he did not deserve. Our deepest shame is not being yoked to a prodigal. Our deepest shame is knowing that Christ was entirely innocent yet brutally crucified, and then discovering *we* are responsible.

As we understand from Scripture, we held the hammer and nails.

But the cross addresses our shame by revealing Christ's shame. The Hebrews passage says, "He despised the shame." Christ was perfect, mistake-free, lawful, loving—and yet he knew shame. How does that work? Well, think about it: Jesus had friends, but no one who stuck by him. One of his best friends denied him; another betrayed him. His followers? Well, one week it was "Hosanna!" and the next it was "Crucify him!"

Jesus knew shame, and he despised it.

BREAKING FREE—DESPISING THE SHAME

"Despised" is an astonishing word choice. What could it mean? Specifically, what could it mean for us—for parents who experience shame each time someone inquiries about their runaway prodigal? Or for the spouse who wakes up under accusation each day because their marriage seems meaningless to their spouse? Or for the thousands of people who are shamed each day by the choices of those who decisively reject their roles and responsibilities?

Jesus despised shame by seeing beyond it. We're not talking about denial here. Christ's abandonment by friends, his rejection by the masses, his being stripped and crucified naked, his degradation in suffering the penalty of the cursed—it was all real. Appallingly real.

And if that shame-fest were not enough, Jesus experienced the ultimate loss of dignity, relationship, and blessing as God's holy wrath was uncorked, and he was left alone crying, "*My God, my God, why have you forsaken me?*" (Matthew 27:46). The scream of forsakenness was also the cry of the shamed.

Christ knew shame. But Christ despised shame because Christ saw beyond shame: "for the joy that was set before him endured the cross, despising the shame" (Hebrews 12:2).

Seeing beyond shame meant Jesus was not controlled by it. Sure, it was painful, but it was powerless to change his identity and to control his future. Shame had no value to him, no voice of influence or authority to name him, to determine who he was. He despised it. We should despise it too.

The path out of shame starts with looking to Jesus. He understands our shame; he's been there. But he also responded to it. Righteously and forcefully. He despised it by seeing beyond it. He saw forward to the time when he would be honored, valued, and esteemed. Not shamed, but "seated at the right hand of the throne of God" (Hebrews 12:2).

Jesus knew that shame wasn't the final word. He knew that the cross meant salvation. He saw beyond the moment into eternity. So should we. We should echo Paul's words in Philippians 3:8:

> Indeed, I count everything as loss because of the sur-
> passing worth of knowing Christ Jesus my Lord. For his sake I
> have suffered the loss of all things and count them as rubbish,
> in order that I may gain Christ.

Shame is an expert on your past. It says you're unclean and unholy. Either you've blown it or your prodigal has, but either way, you're guilty. However the gospel does not just address our past; it also looks to Christ's past. In his past we are reminded that Christ endured the cross and despised the shame so that we could enjoy freedom in the present and hope for the future.

The gospel enables us to shake free from our past because the past doesn't define us. The gospel enables us to look forward to the joy that's before us. The joy that will be ours when the Father pronounces over us, "Well done, good and faithful servant" (Matthew 25:21). The joy that will be ours when we see how God has worked for good through what seemed to be evil. The joy that will be ours when we are finally free from the vestiges of sin.

Shame tries to lock you into the past. Shame tells you that the past governs the future. But the gospel wrestles you free from the death grip of the past and allows you to look ahead, despising the shame that trails you. Shame says you're naked; the gospel says you're clothed with the righteousness of Christ (Philippians 3:9). Shame says you're alone; the gospel says Jesus is here, perfecting your faith (Hebrews 12:2). Shame says you're exiled because of how others see you; the gospel reminds you that you hold the approval of an audience of one, and he's preparing a place for you (John 14:1–3).

Jesus despised shame, rose from the dead, and is seated in heaven (Hebrews 12:2). There he sits praying for us and waiting for us (Romans 8:34). More than that, we have hope in the fact that he won't sit there forever. He's coming back (Revelation 22:20)! And he's all that matters.

LIVING FREE FROM SHAME

Shame is real, but it will not have the final say. So don't let it. Look beyond it to Jesus. Remember, you are not alone. He went before you in suffering shame, yet still despised it. You must do the same.

Jesus can make you clean, and even make you feel clean. Don't listen to the world or your wayward one. Neither are dialed into God right now. Trust in God. Trust his promises. Remember: You serve a Savior who bore your shame all the way to the cross. Don't take it back. Wake up tomorrow and join the chorus.

> *Bearing shame and scoffing rude*
> *In my place condemned he stood.*
> *Sealed my pardon with his blood:*
> *Hallelujah, what a Savior!*[10]

The Wall of Weariness

CHAPTER 10

Fatigue.

Actually, no. Fatigue is close but it depicts only the scab, not the wound. We're talking here about a different kind of depletion. Imagine your life as a pro wrestling ring where emotional exhaustion, mental weariness, and bodily weakness become a tag team who drop in each day with a smack-down. Alarm, breakfast, shower, bruising . . . repeat!

What are we describing here? The collateral damage on a wayward-lover—the friend or family member of one who strays. Prodigals possess a strange power. They suck life out of those who love them. Yes, it's weariness, but it's also something more: a kind of fear-encased, mind-enfeebling, passion-sapping, confidence-wrecking, depression-inciting, bone-tired *exhaustion*. And it's not hard to find the cause. If you love a prodigal, you're always on-call emotionally. If the prodigal is at home, the floors are tiled in eggshells—you either dodge them or crush them in your quest to protect and motivate. If the prodigal is gone, you wait, wonder, and worry about what might happen today. What foolish decisions will he indulge? What influences will she follow? Will he or she be safe?

Then there's the carrot and stick thing. Any positive comment or civil tone, any small sign of life, the smallest flash of courtesy or positive report inflates your heart with a desperate hope that you stand on the threshold of a breakthrough. The last conversation must have worked; God is finally answering your prayers; repentance must be just around the corner!

Then the prodigal gets worse. Your soaring hopes, which skipped upon the clouds only an hour before, lose altitude and come crashing to earth.

Living with a prodigal can inspire a lot of wishful thinking.

So you talk to your prodigal. Oh boy, do you talk! You are convinced that if he or she can just see this one thing, hear this one idea, discuss this one resource . . . "THEN my prodigal will fall to earth, dust off, and set a course for home." And because talk creates the illusion of progress, it becomes a form of self-medication. As others have noted, "The temptation to create conversations that are designed to get the fool 'to see' is stronger than the most addictive drug known to mankind."[11] Yet at the relational bank, prodigals continue to make withdrawals, rarely deposits. So the deficit grows daily, inducing a physical and spiritual malaise that erases joy and colors the world in gloomy shades of gray.

It's an exhausting way to live.

PRODIGALS AND THE HEART

Ralph and Susan understand. They love each other, but you can hardly tell since their teenage daughter Jan decided to drop out of high school. Not to work, but to have more time for her growing "leisure pursuits." Discussing the issue yields little progress since Jan went incommunicado months ago. She now inhabits a sullen world where her family might as well be aliens—people from other planets who invade her space speaking gibberish.

Ralph and Susan are learning a hard lesson: Prodigals reveal every spiritual weakness in the home. Jan's conversational passivity provokes anger in Ralph and fear in Susan. Exasperated by their inability to break through, they turn on each other and are locked in a cycle of accusation and apology. Sleep eludes them; worry consumes them; and energy escapes them. Ralph and Susan are exhausted. Prodigal people exact a toll. Bound up in their waywardness is betrayal, foolishness, lawlessness, self-ishness, and thoughtlessness . . . basically a whole lotta ugly following a never-ending parade of stupid. The result is that you're always bracing against the next blow and steeling yourself in preparation for the next crash.

In Jack Miller's book *Come Back, Barbara* about his daughter's waywardness, his wife captured well the emotional pile-up that prodigal-lovers experience when a prodigal starts to spiral:

> When Barb announced she "was not a Christian and didn't want to be one," my world came crashing in on me. I reacted with anger and fear. I simply couldn't handle it. . . . I felt humiliated and betrayed.[12]

Anger, fear, betrayal, humiliation, these are hard feelings that don't lift quickly. How can a Christian feel so powerless, so anxious, so . . . *weary*?

If this section describes you, prepare yourself for hope. Jesus understands *exactly* how you feel. Not simply because he sym-pathizes (though he does—see Hebrews 4:15), but because Jesus experienced what you are experiencing. And he wants to help ease your weariness so that you can fight courageously for the future of your prodigal.

GOOD NEWS FOR THE WEARY

> Consider him who endured from sinners such hostility against himself, so that you may not grow weary or fainthearted.
>
> *HEBREWS 12:3*

Remember what we learned in the last chapter? Hebrews was written for people who were tired of being sinned against. These people had endured persecution, degradation, and unjust suffering. They were publicly exposed to reproach; they had their property seized; and they courageously identified with scorned saints. God's grace was certainly sufficient, but struggle and exhaustion were their constant companions (Hebrews 10:32–34). According to the book's author, they had "need of endurance" (10:36).

There's never a good time for suffering, but these guys were hardly game-day ready. Just read some of these descriptions: some were "dull of hearing" (Hebrews 5:11), tempted to be "sluggish" (6:12), neglected their meetings (10: 25), and were "weary" and "fainthearted" (12:3). They had "drooping hands" and "weak knees" (12:12). These are pretty poor assets when you're facing a big race.

And they needed to endure.

Specifically, they needed to "run with endurance the race set before [them]" (Hebrews 12:1). Their problem was persecution, not prodigals. But their fundamental need was the same as yours: to get past the pain of how they'd been treated and to refocus on moving forward. To move beyond the rejection, the resentment, the worthless feelings, the fatigue—the whole monotonous headgame that accompanied the absurdities of their situation.

How do they do it? How do we do it? How do we not grow weary or fainthearted?

The writer of Hebrews makes it plain:

"Consider him who endured from sinners such hostility against himself" (12:3).

We know, this sounds pretty loopy. You are probably saying,

"Wait, guys. You mean an important aid to my weariness is to consider how crappy things were for Christ?"

Well, sort of.

Christ's suffering helps our weariness in some specific and powerful ways. But before we share them with you, we want to tell you a story.

THE WAYWARD-WEARY HOME

"It's horrific!"

I (Dave) was barely five minutes into my meeting with a couple we'll call Sal and Leslie, but I could see clearly they were already at a breaking point in dealing with their wayward child, floating somewhere between "scraped raw" and "change our identity and flee the country."

"I mean, it's otherworldly. One conflict just bleeds right into the next one. A minor issue escalates immediately into nuclear war. There's never a break. Never! I mean, the level of chaos in our home is like—" Sal paused, searching for the right words. "I don't know; it's just hard to explain. It's like we're living with some kind of combat fatigue."

Now I've never been in combat, but it wasn't hard to grant them the analogy. Talk to a husband, wife, sibling, or parent who has navigated this prodigal world, and they will often speak of lost days, sleepless nights, relational isolation, and an inconsolable anxiety. Marriages are strained, bank accounts drained, self-confidence maimed . . . all sacrificed to care for the wayward loved one.

Sal and Leslie were battle-weary. They felt sapped, besieged, enfeebled, disoriented, weakened, and wounded. And those were just the physical effects! A more diabolical battle was happening beneath the surface; a skirmish in their soul where the enemy and flesh warred against faith, hope, and love. Remember: Anytime you see a wayward person, family members are often in the shadows wrestling to reconcile the vast difference they are experiencing between *what a family is supposed to be* and *what their family really is.*

What do you tell them? How does Christ's suffering speak to that kind of weariness?

CHRIST'S SUFFERING AND *WHY?*

"Why?" Intractable, inscrutable, unyielding—*why?* is a cross that wayward-lovers must carry. It's one thing to be soul-weary and know the cause. Sam's kid has an illness, and it drains him. Carol lost a loved one, and she's up all night grieving. The cause may be life-altering and earth-shattering, but at least they know what it is. However, a mysterious kind of desperation is inflicted upon the soul when a loved one goes rogue. We ask, "How did we get here? What did we do wrong? What should we do now? Why is this happening to us?"

Occasionally these questions receive clear answers, but often they do not.

Job could relate. Unable to understand why he was suffering, Job cried, "For he crushes me with a tempest and multiplies my wounds without cause" (Job 9:17). Like many of us do when we are faced with piercing affliction, Job looked up at the heavens. He felt alone and said, "I cry out to you, God, but you do not answer" (Job 30:20 NIV).

Multiplied wounds without cause. If you have loved a wayward person, you get it. When someone you love goes wayward and you don't know the cause, the suffering and fatigue seem irrational and arbitrary. We ride the curved back of the question mark straight into a wall of exhaustion. One woman who watched her husband deteriorate from Godward to wayward said, "You pound on 'why' because you think the answer reveals the mysterious virus causing the problems. You think *if I had obeyed God this wouldn't be happening*. You ask relentless questions about yourself, your marriage, and look for what you may have missed. It ends with you collapsed into a heap, exhausted and defeated by the question!"

For some, "Why?" is the most wearisome question on earth.

But according to the author of Hebrews, Christ's suffering does not leave why unanswered. "Consider him who endured from sinners such hostility against himself, so that you may not grow weary or fainthearted" (12:3). It's an odd prescription for someone who's suffering: Be comforted by someone who suffered worse. But this is not merely like taking a guy with pneumonia into the cancer ward to provide him with some perspective on how bad things could really be. It's more than that.

The cross helps make sense of the weariness of why.

Christ's suffering at the hands of wayward sinners reminds us that gigantic good can come from the dreadfully bad things that exhaust us. Let us explain. Imagine for a moment that you are standing before the cross while the Son of Man hangs suspended between heaven and earth. Flogged beyond recognition, exhausted beyond comprehension, a mass of bloodied flesh nailed to a tree. Jesus gasps for air, practically suffocating from the torment. It is utterly horrific.

Imagine further that you had been present for the prior three years of Christ's earthly ministry. What did you see? You were astounded by his power to heal; you marveled over his supernatural works; you delighted at his wit and wisdom; you were convicted by the marks of his righteousness. Everyone knew they were in the presence of a phenom. No living being had ever seen or heard anyone like him.

But now . . . THIS! You stand before the cross bewildered, unreservedly flummoxed, totally stupefied! After all, the one who is so godly, so wise, so beautiful, so other-worldly *is dying a gruesome death.* The most perfect being ever born of a woman—the Son of Man, the Great I Am, the Savior—is being murdered by wicked men. He is dying. Soon he will be gone forever. If you could somehow find the words to convey your horror, they would likely escape through your clenched teeth as, "Why?" With a tone that's equal parts anger, confusion, and despair, you cry, "Is this how God deals with the righteous? Is THIS how God rewards those who follow him wholeheartedly? Is *THIS* justice?"

"It's insane," you say. "How can good ever come of this?"

But wait! In less than a weekend, this spectacle of suffering will reveal a great miracle. The cross and resurrection reveal, once and for all, the immeasurable, unfathomable love God has for the wayward. At the cross, amid the blood, anger, and hostility, it all seems so arbitrary, so useless, so wasted. But what we really behold is the subversive work of divine salvation where God's justice is vindicated, sin's penalty is paid, and God's enemy is decisively vanquished. The midday darkness settling over the land is actually the dawn of a new day of power.

Here's our point: When you're looking at Jesus on the cross, things look pretty bad. The elusive *why* remains unanswered. You see only the irrational hostility, the misery of hopelessness, the agony of defeat—another hero whose young life is being snuffed out. Life seems so empty.

But the appearance is not the substance.

In the drama of Golgotha, God is not merely the backstage director ensuring everything goes according to script. He is the drama's author, existing entirely outside of the production. He knows the beginning and the end. He wrote every part played and determined every word spoken. And his intentions are always loving and good.

In the end, Job realized this too. God was not absent. He wasn't asleep on the job. He answered Job's cries by reminding him that he is God, that he is not surprised, and that he is in control. The good news is that God wrote your family drama, whatever it may be. And his intentions have always been loving and good! We see the trees; God sees the forest. Does your situation look pretty bad? God wants to plant some encouragement deep within your heart. The cross stands as an eternal reminder that there's always, *always* an inconceivable good at work even in the worst events of your life. The author says so, and he wrote the script.

CHRIST'S SUFFERING AND OUR FATIGUE

Fatigue isolates. All relational energy gets pumped into survival. Combine this fact with the shame factor or the "If only I had done this" factor, and you often see people alone in navigating their path of dealing with a wayward loved one. In the echo chamber of solitude, it doesn't take long for dangerous thoughts to surface: *No one can relate to the pressures I feel; no one understands the absurdities within our family; no one gets what it's like for me to struggle daily with all this sin.*

Actually, someone does. Jesus wants to encourage you from his experience. "In your struggle against sin you have not yet resisted to the point of shedding your blood" (Hebrews 12:4).

Tucked in the interior of a secluded garden, Jesus knelt to pray. The stress was enormous as he prepared to become God's sacrificial lamb. Great drops of blood appeared on his forehead and streamed down his face—a bodily response to the crushing burden of sin that would be placed upon him. Denial, betrayal, torture, crucifixion, forsakenness, all of was it just a few hours away. He knew the hearts of men (John 2:24–25). This would not end well.

Christ is an expert witness on what it means to be overwhelmed when loving wayward people. "My Father, if it be possible, let this cup pass from me," he said. But then, as though catching himself, he whispered, "nevertheless, not as I will, but as you will" (Matthew 26:39).

Jesus sweat blood. He felt the strain; he fought back the temptations; he endured the scorn and humiliation of fools. Then he died, a bloody corpse dangling from a cross. Jesus struggled against the sins of others. He resisted any escape to the point of shedding his blood. "Violence and death," says P. T. O'Brien, "thus represent the supreme degree of opposition in a struggle against sin."[3]

Jesus was not only the pioneer of our faith, but he was also the pioneer in our temptations and struggles with wayward people. You are not alone; you are not crazy; your situation is not incomprehensible; your fatigue is not unbearable; your suffering is not intolerable—Jesus has gone before you in this experience. He gets it. In fact, Jesus sweat and spilled blood to ensure "that we may receive mercy and find grace to help in time of need" (Hebrews 4:16).

Are you weary? Take heart. Jesus understands, and he knows exactly what you need. Christ knows you're tempted to lash out. He understands why it's hard to sleep. Jesus knows what it's like to feel forsaken. Don't give up. You can bear your prodigal's sins a bit longer without striking back.

But we are not just talking about surviving an endurance test. You can do practical things to really fortify your perseverance. Think of them as endurance boosters:

1. *Don't neglect your physical health.* Exercise, eating, and sleeping are not dispensable. Loving prodigals is a marathon, not a sprint. Neglecting life, eating, or physical disciplines is like adding ankle weights for the race. You can be more easily wearied, worn-out, and tempted to withdraw. Don't do it. Keep moving.

2. *Don't neglect your spiritual health.* Take time to read and meditate on God's promises. Confess fear, control, anger . . . then repeat. A season with a prodigal is like living at a rock concert—the music is always jacked up to a hundred decibels. Spiritual disciplines mute the racket and raise the gospel-decibels so you can hear from your Father in heaven. This is a defining moment in your life. Fast, journal, write out your prayers, and recruit a band of fellow believers to help. Your prodigal is not going down without a fight.

3. *Don't neglect your emotional health.* You are experiencing much sadness right now; take time to grieve. Talk with close friends and leaders. Let fellowship be an oasis in the prodigal desert. Tell them how you feel, and ask them to pray. Even though he knows, tell God exactly how you feel too. Every day. Look to the Psalms when you don't know how to put your emotions into words.

4. *Don't neglect your relational health.* When life gets hard, people tend to withdraw. You likely feel alone and isolated. That's exactly what our enemy wants. Don't give him the upper hand. Make sure you are continuing to connect relationally with your church members. Spend time with other Christians. Seek out those who have suffered similarly. Ask them for help. Find out what fed them. Confess your sins to others as they surface. Trust God by relying on those who love you.

5. *Don't neglect your intellectual health.* Push your thoughts beyond your prodigal. Read biographies; work through a Bible study; do your hobby. These activities are not frivolous or meaningless; they will supply your soul through back channels. You are still human; you still have interests—don't let your world shrink to the size of your problems. Feeding your sanity will help you keep it.

6. *Don't neglect your family health.* You are a spouse, a son or daughter, a parent, a sibling. Yes, the wayward one is gone, but everyone else remains. Confusion and pain abound. They need you, and they need your strength. The loss of one need not produce other casualties. Get busy loving and caring for the rest. Go out on dates with your spouse. Serve your sister or brother. Gather the family to pray. Let those you love see the faith you hold.

7. *Don't neglect your history.* This is not the first time you've suffered. You bear other scars. Yet God has always been faithful. Remember back to the other times he came through. Remember how your fears prophesied your doom, but God delivered you. Remember God raises the

dead! He's done it in your soul; he's done it in your past; he can do it in your prodigal.

Above all, fight to keep the right perspective. Fleeing to Christ will help. He's a great reminder that, "You have not yet resisted to the point of shedding blood" (Hebrews 12:4).

CHRIST'S SUFFERING AND DOING GOOD

Jesus loved prodigals to the very end. His statement "It is finished" (John 19:30) was not an admission of defeat but a declaration of success. Christ had overcome sin. Love won. Forgiveness is available. Prodigals can come home.

But their coming home can take time. Prodigals move slowly.

Recently I (Dave) spoke to a woman who said she has been seeking to love her prodigal child who now lives in another city. She supplied a number of ways she was reaching out. It was a pretty impressive, intentional, love-saturated list. She asked me what else she might do. I simply said, "And let us not grow weary of doing good, for in due season we will reap, if we do not give up" (Galatians 6:9).

She got the point. Your prodigal is not your enemy. Giving up is your enemy. Weariness is your enemy. Thank God that in certain situations, a period of waywardness can be short. May there be more! But most prodigal stories are more like that of the son in Luke 15:11–32, a saga that spans the time it took to travel far, indulge much, deposit consequences, withdraw consequences, collapse under consequences, get a clue, and then travel slowly home.

Here's the formula for waiting: Buckle up; don't grow weary; do good; don't give up!

Most importantly, don't miss the promise: "For in due season, we will reap" (Galatians 6:9). "Due season" is not here yet. "For everything there is a season, and a time for every matter under heaven" (Ecclesiastes 3:1). Now is not the season or the time. You will reap; just don't give up.

MARRY A WHORE

> When the LORD first spoke through Hosea, the LORD said to Hosea, "Go, take to yourself a wife of whoredom and have children of whoredom, for the land commits great whoredom by forsaking the LORD."
>
> *HOSEA 1:2*

You know a story is going to be saucy when it starts with "Go marry a whore!" But God wanted to show Hosea and us a little something about love. Hosea obeyed and made Gomer his wife. He married a wayward woman.

As we've seen, a strong impulse that motivates the wayward heart is the desire to flee—from God, from roles, from responsibilities, from consequences. Gomer fled. Hosea let her go in a display of rugged love. But this story is also appallingly tragic. In the midst of it comes one of the most astonishing passages in Scripture.

> And the LORD said to me, "Go again, love a woman who is loved by another man and is an adulteress, even as the LORD loves the children of Israel, though they turn to other gods and love cakes of raisins." So I bought her for fifteen shekels of silver and a homer and a lethech of barley.
>
> *HOSEA 3:1–2*

Go again. Hosea went once; now he's called to do go yet again. *Go and pursue her; go and redeem her; go and do good!*

Hosea went. Gomer was redeemed. The point was made. God's love endures. God's love perseveres. God's love is longsuffering and patient. God does not give up. Aren't you glad God doesn't grow weary of you? Aren't you grateful he never gives up? He doesn't give up, and neither should you.

Maybe you're married to Gomer right now, and you must let her go, only to take her back again someday. Maybe Gomer is your teenager, or a close friend who's preparing for flight. Letting go does not mean forsaking love. Letting go does not mean abandoning mercy. Letting go means rugged love. And rugged love never gives up.

DON'T GIVE UP!

We don't have all the reasons why God allows prodigals to wander, but we do know this: Through the present mess, God is working. And if you feel like you're dying each day, be of good cheer. Remember the promise in Psalm 30:5, "Weeping may tarry for the night, but joy comes with the morning."

In the fullness of time, dark nights end, cold winters subside, and fruit comes forth. We live to laugh again because the one we rely upon is the one "who endured from sinners such hostility against himself" (Hebrews 12:3).

We know you're tired. Don't give up. Christ endured. And through his grace, you will too.

Faith for Barren Times

I f you've made it to this final chapter, then we've traveled quite a distance together. We've looked at what it means to love someone with a rugged love, and we've learned what it means to face the difficult decision to let a loved one go. We've walked the shadowy valleys of shame and weariness. If you are walking the road of wayward lovers, hopefully you've discovered that grace not only saves you; it rescues you from dark places and keeps you moving forward.

But there's one last section of path before we reach the end of the journey, and it begins with news that will be, at least initially, hard to hear: *A prodigal rarely returns quickly, so you must prepare for a long, slow wait.*

If your heart is sinking as you read this, stay with us. God is faithful to his promises and our prayers, but his plan usually follows a timetable that's gradual and inscrutable. In the absence of fruit, change, repentance, or even civility, God wants us to trust him. Even when all the circumstances offer little hope. God wants to give us faith when everything around us looks barren. Just like he's done for others.

BARREN—A STORY

He was seventy-five years old. His name, Abram, literally means "father of many"—a rather stabbing irony for a man with no kids.

Even so, he was wealthy, healthy, happy, and comfortably surrounded by family—until God spoke.

"Go from your country and your kindred and your father's house to the land that I will show you. And I will make of you a great nation" (Genesis 12:1–2). If your imagination works like ours, you can imagine Abram thinking, *Great nation? From a man with no kids? How does that work?*

Abram obeyed God. He uprooted his family, which included his wife, a nephew, many servants, innumerable livestock, and all his earthly possessions, and he went forth, "not knowing where he was going" (Hebrews 11:8). And as he journeyed, he waited. Every week, every month, every year, he waited for God to fulfill his divine promise.

Fast-forward several years. The promise seems dead in the water, still unfulfilled. It's not hard to imagine Abram in an anguished state. He still has no children, which means he has no heir. *Great nation?* he may have thought, *What's all this business about a great nation? At this point, I'd settle for a good neighborhood with a nice cul-de-sac. Where's the great nation?*

In response to Abram's wonderings and wanderings, God takes him outside and bids him to look up to the heavens at the stars. Then God speaks these eternal words: "So shall your offspring be" (Genesis 15:5). Scripture says that Abram believed God, and his belief was counted to him as righteousness (Romans 4:3).

Now all of this might be swell if the story ended there. You know, a typical blockbuster storyline—characters, setting, plot, conflict, and . . . resolution! But God speaking to Abram was not the resolution. It was actually the start of another conflict. Because Abram was about to encounter the torturous tutorial of a long, slow wait.

The first couple of years probably weren't so bad. But time has a way of eroding both memory and faith. After seven or eight years of waiting for God to fulfill his promise, we can imagine Abram second-guessing himself, asking, "Did God really give me his word? Did he really speak to me? Did he really appear?"

His circumstances certainly weren't changing. His wife, Sarai, was still barren. Abram's body was decaying. Was God going to come through on his promise?

Sarai became restless too. Thinking that God's promise could never be fulfilled through her old, barren body, Sarai pushed her servant Hagar onto Abram. Abram capitulated, and Ishmael was conceived. But Ishmael was not the promised one.

Another fourteen years pass.

To reaffirm his promise, God again visits Abram. He changes his name from Abram, "father of many," to Abraham, "father of a multitude." God also changes Sarai's name to Sarah.

At this point, Abraham isn't just old; he is ninety-nine. He is "remember back when we used to have sex" old. Sarah isn't exactly maternity material either. She is well beyond child-bearing years, way past menopause. The window of opportunity for having kids is closed. They could claim one son, but the child isn't Sarah's, and the child certainly isn't the promised one.

How long would they wait?

One year later—twenty-five years after the initial promise—Isaac is born.

If you love someone who is straying, just ponder that waiting period. Not because you need to settle in for a bumpy ride over the next quarter-century. Not at all. We want to get you thinking about how even the Bible's "elite" had to wait for God to fulfill promises of life.

BARREN—A SCRIPTURE

In Romans 4:18–21, Paul tells us more about Abraham and Sarah's wait:

> In hope he believed against hope, that he should become the father of many nations, as he had been told, "So shall your offspring be." He did not weaken in faith when he considered his own body, which was as good as dead (since he was about a hundred years old), or when he considered the barrenness of Sarah's womb. No unbelief made him waver concerning the promise of God, but he grew strong in his faith as he gave glory to God, fully convinced that God was able to do what he had promised.

While Romans 4 is certainly about faith that saves, it also serves as an instruction manual for the faith we need each day. All of the ingredients for a daily, God-pleasing faith are present in Abraham's faith, which is why the author of Hebrews uses Abraham's example to call believers to persevere through faith in God. Because the faith that justifies sparks a faith for daily life. The faith that justifies carries along with it faith that helps us persevere in life.

If you want to live patiently waiting for God to act in your prodigal, you need to understand this kind of faith. So let's take a few moments and dissect Abraham's faith.

BELIEVING THE PROMISES

In describing Abraham, Paul makes it clear that true faith begins with believing God's promises: "In hope he believed against hope, that he should become the father of many nations, as he had been told, 'So shall your offspring be'" (Romans 4:18).

God had told Abraham that he would be a father. Abraham responded by trusting that God would do exactly as he promised. True faith invests trust in the words of God and stands on them as guarantees of a future reality. Abraham's trust was bigger than having an experience with God. His faith didn't rest on the fact that he encountered angels, strolled around heaven, or had any supernatural experience with God.

The problem with "experiences" is that our memory of their impact fades quickly. The Israelites had an incredible, life-altering, supernatural experience of God at the Red Sea, and yet they soon forgot. Just a short time later, they were pining for Egypt, protesting God's plan, and partying in front of a golden calf.

Memories, even of the most magnificent earthly experiences, fade. I (Dave) know they fade for me. A few years back, Kimm and I were in our small group meeting, and our anniversary was just a few days away. Knowing our anniversary was coming, our small group leader causally said, "Hey, give us a memory of your wedding day."

For some inexplicable reason the question caught us totally by surprise. "Ahhh . . ." I bought some time with the hopes that my brain might reset. Wedding day, wedding song, wedding—what, *come on brain!* My wedding day—the most significant day of my life apart from my conversion! And my mind desperately searched the database and got nothing! I looked down at my hand and saw my wedding ring; yes, I was definitely married. But for some reason, there was giant gap in my memory-file for that day.

Memories fade.

Here's the point: Abraham didn't stand on a vague memory of a spiritual experience. Rather, he drove a stake of confidence into the words God had spoken to him. He tethered himself not to a fleeting, forgettable experience, but to the unshakable word of God.

We too have promises from God. The Bible is a warehouse of promises. If we are not working in the warehouse of God's Word, we simply won't grow in faith. Romans 10:17 makes this clear, "So faith comes from hearing, and hearing through the word of Christ."

Imagine for a moment that your prodigal is gone. Like the son in Luke 15, he or she has left for a distant country and is now spending money on a life that grieves your soul. Your prodigal parties; you worry. Anxiety is your constant companion. During the day, you feel it as a detached sense of unrest, a floating feeling that touches down, sometimes as guilt or maybe anger, and other times as plain dread. You awaken in the middle of the night, your brain turning over contingencies, or connecting the dots between your prodigal's choices and your guilt. *What if she's hurt and needs help? How will he support himself? What did we do to produce these problems? How could they do this to us?*

In those fearful moments, true faith doesn't say, "God, I'm feeling anxious. Appear to me in a vision!" No, faith says, "God has revealed himself in his Word, so I will go to the Scriptures and listen to the promises of God." Maybe you grab hold of Philippians 4:6–7:

> Do not be anxious about anything, but in everything by prayer and supplication with thanksgiving let your requests be made known to God. And the peace of God, which surpasses all understanding, will guard your hearts and your minds in Christ Jesus.

What a great promise! If we pray when we're anxious, God

supplies peace. Give Scripture the microphone and turn up the volume.

Are your days like ours? Every day, a variety of voices speak to us. Our fears speak. Our circumstances speak. Our enemies speak. Our suffering speaks. Faith trusts what God says about the future more than what those voices say in the present. If you love one who is straying, you must constantly be asking, "What voices matter most? What voices speak loudest to me right now? Are my feelings speaking loudest? My circumstances? Or am I hearing God's Word?"

Paul informs us that Abraham had to wrestle through these questions. Abraham eventually became "fully convinced that God was able to do what he promised" (Romans 4:21). But let's face it. Abraham didn't start there; "he grew strong in his faith" (Romans 4:20).

We want you to think about one word there. Abraham *grew* in faith. This means he didn't start out believing God's promises. Abraham was just like you and us. He had to struggle and fight to get to a place of faith. But eventually, he became convinced that God could do what he said.

How did Abraham arrive at a place where his heart was fully convinced? He believed God's Word. He staked all his faith on the bare words of God. D. Martyn Lloyd Jones said, "There is always this naked element in faith. It does not ask for proofs, it does not seek them; in a sense, it does not need them. Faith is content with the bare word of God."[14]

God-pleasing faith believes the "bare word" of God.

EMBRACING THE CIRCUMSTANCES

People fleeing God can end up in some ugly places. Drugs, crime, lying, pregnancy, raging fits of profanity—their rebellion connects them to the dark underbelly of the community. Things can get pretty bad, which also means life can get very sad. John Piper once said, "A son is not a father's only life investment, but there is none like it, and when it fails, there is no sorrow like this sorrow."[5]

Some spouses and parents develop a "darkness sensitivity" where they're mentally and physically averse to seeing how far their loved one has fallen. It's a sophisticated form of denial created to protect them from the pain of seeing the dark truth. The two things we must know about this form of denial is first, it's completely understandable, and second, it's unmitigated unbelief.

God-pleasing faith embraces the seemingly hopelessness of the circumstances.

In Romans 4:19, we read that Abraham "did not weaken in faith when he considered his own body, which was as good as dead, (since he was about a hundred years old)"; nor did his faith weaken "when he considered the barrenness of Sarah's womb." You know what we love about this description? We love how it links *faith to reality*. Abraham was not in denial about the problems. He did no spin control; he did not dump the evidence because it made the situation look hopeless. On the contrary, he makes an unvarnished assessment of how bad things really were. In fact, verse 18 says of Abraham, "In hope he believed against hope." That's just another way of saying that things seemed pretty hopeless. The raw truth was that Abraham's body was as good as dead, and Sarah's womb was totally barren.

In the name of faith, some believers fudge the numbers. They say things like, "My daughter said the drugs weren't hers; she needs our trust right now," or "My husband feels that how he spends his time is none of my business; he needs my understanding right now." Our fears can confine our inquiries. The truth is too frightening, too painful.

But isn't Romans 4 a refreshing passage? Rather than indulging the unbelief behind his fear, Abraham took an honest look at where things stood. He considered his circumstances, and once he had, he was able to sincerely admit that things were bad, very bad. It's like he said, "You know, as I look at myself and my wife, things look pretty dead." And yet, Abraham didn't weaken in faith when he considered his own deadness or her barrenness.

Hopelessness was the reality. But faith uses reality as a starting point for God's activity.

Think about what Romans 4 is saying about Abraham and Sarah. We look at Abraham; things seems impossible. We look at Sarah; a pregnancy seems incomprehensible. Everywhere we look is dead. No seed, no hope, no way, no . . . *life*. It's as if circumstances have convened as a jury to return this verdict upon Abraham and Sarah: Impossible! There's no way this son thing can happen. Do you see the point? *Abraham believed in God when there was no life.* He trusted when it seemed like there was no way forward, when it seemed like God's promise was in the realm of the impossible.

You're likely reading this book because you live in circumstances where, after a gut-level, candid analysis, you see only barrenness. You see your prodigal's life, and you see the consequences of sin. And when you're brutally honest, you see no change. No interest in the Lord. No interest in the family. No interest in truth. No spiritual life. Despite all your prayers and love and labor, your prodigal still appears to be dead.

You think, *This person has been given so much by God, yet there seems to be so little fruit for him.* There's no zeal, no heart, no interest, no life. All you see is barrenness.

Who can relate to these circumstances?

Abraham can relate—to the tune of twenty-five years of total barrenness. God brought Abraham and Sarah to the point where they were physically unable to produce any sort of life. Abraham was a hundred, and Sarah was ninety. His body? As good as dead. Her body? Barren. And these facts were all placed intentionally in the text. God brought Abraham and Sarah to a place where it was evident to them, and everyone else, that their situation was beyond human remedy. If anything was going to change, it had to be caused by some kind of outside, supernatural intervention. It had to be an act of God and God alone.

Friends, we don't always get it, but sometimes God uses prodigals to return us to the very lesson we learned at conversion: change comes from God alone. Our salvation was not of us; our ongoing sanctification is not ultimately by us; and our final security is not through us.

Maybe you've been waiting many years for your prodigal to return to God. You've been praying and waiting, and you're beginning to feel desperate. Feeling desperate isn't a bad thing. It can be a step toward shedding self-confidence so you rely only on God.

That's what happened to Abraham. He crossed a bridge from a view that was circumstance-centered to a faith that was promise-centered. Because of this transformation, Paul says of him, "He did not weaken in faith when he considered his own body. No unbelief made Abraham waver concerning the promises of God" (Romans 4:19–20).

The situation was bad. But Abraham embraced it.

SUSTAINING THE TRUST

Abraham's story gets even more intriguing, and if you love one who is straying, even more relevant. *Abraham believed long before his circumstances changed.* In Romans 4:20, Paul says of Abraham, "No distrust made him waver concerning the promise of God, but he grew strong in his faith as he gave glory to God."

Consider this. Abraham's faith came alive even though his body was dead. His dark night of the soul became the place where God schooled his faith. Abraham met God when there was no life in him, which eventually brought his faith to life. He met God in the pain of barrenness.

Most often, our faith sparks only when we see some hopeful sign in our circumstances. Can you relate? We're struggling with unbelief about our prodigal situation. But then we suddenly see some hopeful sign. Our prodigal asks a question, or says a prayer, or extends some unexpected kindness. The surprise causes us to think, *See, God is at work!* We saw a sign; now our faith can come out of hiding.

The problem is that true faith doesn't synch to circumstances. It synchs to promises. Just like Abraham's did.

Abraham had no hopeful signs. Change took place within him long before any circumstantial improvements. And if he was like us, we're sure that internal change didn't happen quickly. We're sure he passed through all the phases we do: denial of circumstances (It can't really be this bad!); then anger (I can't believe it's this bad!); then demands that God change the circumstances (If you really love me, you'll change this!); then acceptance, where faith is born (Maybe God is at work in this); and finally anticipation of how God is going to fulfill his promise and actually giving him glory in advance of that fulfillment (Lord, thank you for how you are at work in this!). Abraham began to stand on the Word of God and anticipate something from God long before his circumstances changed.

If you are suffering as a prodigal-lover, you have joined the ranks of many throughout history who have waited years for their loved ones to come to their senses (Luke 15:17). Abraham's story reminds us to wait patiently for God's promises. Remember the name given to him at birth: Abram, "father of many." When he was a kid, this was surely a source of pride, a kind of proclamation of a prodigious future.

So Abram took a bride; they started a life together; *and the kids didn't come.* A year passed. Two years. Five. Still no kids. Abram's Facebook profile read: "Father of many—still no kids."

How many times did Abram meet new people only to have them infer from his name that his quiver was overflowing?

"What's your name?"

"Abram."

"Congratulations! *Abram*—father of many! Where are your children?"

"I . . . have . . . none."

Thousands of times. "I . . . have . . . none."

Imagine the shame of Abram and Sarai. Imagine the awkward conversations with neighbors and family members. Imagine the pain they experienced every time they had to say that word *none.* It got so embarrassing that eventually Sarai sent Abram into the arms of another woman.

Yet in God's mysterious, often perplexing plan, he used all the pain and confusion and difficult circumstances to do a transformational work in Abraham—a work so deep that Abraham was ultimately willing to sacrifice the son he'd waited twenty-five years to father. God worked so comprehensively in Abraham that he loved no one more than God. No one Abraham trusted more than God. Nothing he treasured more than God's Word. God forged Abraham into a man of whom Paul could say, "No unbelief made him waver concerning the promise of God" (Romans 4:20).

BARREN—THE CLAIM

How are you doing in your season of waiting for God to work in your prodigal? Are you waiting patiently for God to work? Or have you been busy conceiving an Ishmael? Ishmael was the son of a slave. In Galatians 4:23, Paul says Ishmael symbolizes a child of the flesh. He represents a self-sufficient choice that displaces God and says, "You know what, God? I'm done! I'm done waiting. I'm done trusting—I'll do this myself!"

Ishmaels are conceived when impatience marries unbelief.

Maybe you feel as though the daily conflict with your prodigal husband is just not worth the hassle. You are tempted to say, "Let him say what he wants and do what he wants. I just don't have the energy to fight this battle right now. I'll deal with it later. I'll accommodate him just to keep the peace. After all, a little enabling is better than a broken family." But eighteen months later, the dream of peace will be an illusion and you become the family carpet for both husband and kids. Your Ishmael will stare you in the face each day as a type of reminder of the fruitlessness of your own efforts. We've been there.

But if this scenario describes or discourages you, we want you to consider something important. Abraham is presented in Scripture as someone who got faith right, *and Ishmael is embedded in the middle of his story.* Abraham is not held up as someone who was perfect. Rather, he points forward to the One who would come—the One who would obey God's law perfectly and believe God's Word completely. Abraham points forward to the coming of Jesus.

Because Jesus lived a perfect life and died a substitutionary death and because he rose from the dead and ascended into heaven, he now has the power and authority to redeem us from the mistakes we've made and the sins we've committed. He can actually work in and through the Ishmaels we've conceived through our unbelief.

Think about it. Our fleshly choices—those times when we failed to trust God—need no longer define us. This means we don't need to spend the rest of our lives trying to atone for our own mistakes and sins. We can trust in the atonement of Jesus.

Still, we all live in a real world where our Ishmaels may live on day after day. We may even be reminded of the catastrophic choices we've made. But here's the thing: Our mistakes and sins are written into a bigger story that passes through the cross that redeems us, despite the past, despite our sins, despite our mistakes, despite our failures, despite our Ishmaels.

Of course, you aren't a sinless spouse or a perfect parent. But you trust in a sinless and perfect Savior. And that's enough. Abraham trusted too. Trusting God was how he was able to grow strong in faith, give glory to God, and be fully convinced that God could do what he promised.

DON'T GIVE UP—GIVE GLORY TO GOD!

As we close this book, we want to invite you to respond like Abraham. Give glory to God right here and right now, fully convinced that God is able to do what he promised. Abraham didn't wait until there was a significant change in his situation; he began to worship while he waited. Abraham gave glory to God even when there was no life.

May God help us to see him so clearly that his promises are more real than our circumstances! And may this happen so we can give glory to God right here and right now,

not because our circumstances have changed,

but because our faith *has*.

CHAPTER 12

Grace Wins!

He is dead!" the bishop whispered. His words hung in the air like a damp fog, shrouding John's soul with dread.

"How, and by what kind of death?" whispered John.

"He is dead . . . to God!" the bishop replied, "for he turned wicked and abandoned, and at last became a robber. And now, instead of the church, he haunts the mountain with a band like himself."

■ ■ ■

This exchange comes from the middle of an extraordinary story taken from the pages of church history. It relates an incident in the life of John, one of the close disciples of Jesus and the final apostle. It comes to us through the writings of the Roman historian Eusebius[16] and was originally included in a book by Clement of Alexandria.[17]

The story begins when John returns from exile on the isle of Patmos (as related in the book of Revelation). John visits the city of Smyrna and meets a young man "of powerful physique, of pleasing appearance, and of ardent temperament." This young man has great leadership potential, and he impresses the aging apostle so much that John makes special arrangements with the church bishop for his upkeep and training. The bishop agrees that the young man can live with him, reaping the benefits of his personal training and care. Certainly, this was an exceptional opportunity for an aspiring leader, and the young man applies himself most diligently. At first.

It's hard to know why the young man began to wander. Our sinful desires are something of a mystery, defying both love and logic (see 2 Thessalonians 2:7). The young man, despite having godly mentors, eventually falls under the corrupting influence of his peers. Eusebius writes: "At first they enticed him by costly entertainments; then, when they went forth at night for robbery, they took him with them, and finally they demanded that he should unite with them in some greater crime."

Which he did. Again. And again. The sin felt exciting at first. Then it became easy, then entertaining. The young man "rushed the more violently down into the depths," and with each rebellious act, he secretly despaired of his salvation in Christ. Finally, assuming that he was truly lost to God, the young man formed "a band of robbers (and) became a bold bandit-chief, the most violent, most bloody, most cruel of them all." Put in today's context, we might describe him as the head of a gang, a notorious street thug or drug dealer. He wore the colors and rolled as a professional banger. If the wayward life was a multi-level marketing business, this young man had earned his diamond membership within months of joining.

Time passes. The apostle John returns to the church and inquires about the young man. At this point, the bishop shares the sad words that we read at the beginning of this chapter: "He is dead . . . to God!"

If you love a prodigal, you understand these words. We suspect that little has changed in your situation since you started reading this book. To you, your loved one may seem dead to God, and your relationship may be no better, possibly even worse, than it was when you began reading. We want to leave you with a final encouragement: Don't give up. With God there is always hope.

Prodigals provoke a response, even by their absence. Upon hearing the report about the young man, the apostle John "rent his clothes and beat his head with great lamentation." When someone we love is lost in sin, we grieve. Our wardrobe and appearance no longer matter.

But God's love is greater than our grief.

John turns from his grief and calls for a horse. He asks where he might find the young man and his gang. Riding directly to that location, he is seized by the members of the gang and taken prisoner. Eusebius tells us that John "neither fled nor made entreaty, but cried out, 'For this did I come; lead me to your captain.'"

Never in his wildest dreams had the young man thought that an apostle of Jesus would come after him, riding out to seek him on his turf. So when the young man sees John, he flees in shame. Eusebius describes how John responded: "But John, forgetting his age, pursued him with all his might, crying out, 'Why, my son, dost thou flee from me, thine own father, unarmed, aged? Pity me, my son; fear not; thou hast still hope of life . . . I will willingly endure thy death as the Lord suffered death for us. For thee will I give up my life. Stand, believe; Christ hath sent me.'"

The young man slows. Then he stops. His guilt and shame are so heavy on his heart that he cannot lift his head. And at that moment, a divine power stirs desires long dead. Irresistible glimmers of grace break over his heart, carrying rays of sweet contrition. Eusebius tells us that the young man broke down and "embraced (John), making confession with lamentations as he was able, baptizing himself a second time with tears."

If this was a Hollywood movie, the screen would fade to black at this moment. The prodigal repents, the church rejoices, and everyone lives happily ever after. But Hollywood is not real life, and the road stretches out miles beyond that moment of repentance. Real life begins at the moment of repentance, and a prodigal needs help knowing how to come home and how to stay home.

So why do we end our book with this story about the apostle John? Because of what happens next: "But John . . . .with copious prayers, and struggling together with him in continual fastings, and subduing his mind by various utterances, he did not depart, as they say, until he had restored him to the church, furnishing a great example of true repentance and a great proof of regeneration, a trophy of a visible resurrection."

Yes, it's a classic testimony: a gang leader repents and becomes a "trophy of a visible resurrection." But notice that reaching this point took time and required copious prayers and fasting. John struggled together with the young man, speaking truth to his mind. But in the end, the wayward soul can come home again. Rugged love not only covers the multitude of sins (1 Peter 4:8); it stays around to rumble until the resurrection is complete.

We share this story to remind you that God has been doing this kind of work for centuries. Your prodigal situation is not new or unexpected. God is in the business of saving prodigals—it's what he does best. And his grace is magnified in this work.

Do you feel a spark of hope after reading this story? We hope so. God uses stories like this to kindle embers buried deep within us. Hope starts with an exchange, a swapping of our perspective for God's. It comes through those moments of crucifixion when, as Paul described, "we felt that we had received the sentence of death" (2 Corinthians 1:9a). But in those times, we make a decision. We suspend judgment upon God and in faith believe that he has a purpose for our pain: "But that was to make us rely not on ourselves but on God who raises the dead" (2 Corinthians 1:9b). Whatever your circumstances, know that God is shifting your reliance—relocating it from a frail and fallen source (ourselves!) to the "God who raises the dead." The spark grows to a flame as our reliance upon God grows. We dare to believe that his resurrecting power is not confined to the ministry of the apostle John. The death of our marriage, the loss of our son or daughter, the rebellion of a friend or family member is not the end of the story—God raises the dead!

As you finish this book, remember that God's rugged love carries his resurrecting power. And if you feel like you're dying each day, be encouraged. "Weeping may tarry for the night, but joy comes with the morning" (Psalm 30:5). In the fullness of time, dark nights end, cold winters subside, and hope heals. We live to laugh again because the One who showed us rugged love empowers us to exercise it. Even in the pain of letting go, we remember the power that links the apostle John's story to our own: *The God we rely upon is the God who raises the dead.*

Notes

1. Dan Allender and Tremper Longman, *Bold Love* (Colorado Springs: NavPress, 1992), 264.

2. C. S. Lewis, *The Four Loves* (New York: Harcourt, Brace, 1988), 121.

3. Robert Cheong, *God Redeeming His Bride* (Fearn, Scotland: Christian Focus, 2013), 10.

4. While we subscribe to the view that remarriage is an option for those who are deserted by a spouse who acts willfully and irremediably, a discussion or apologetic for our position is outside of the scope of this project.

5. Jim Newheiser and Elyse Fitzpatrick, *You Never Stop Being a Parent* (Phillipsburg, N.J.: P&R, 2010), 112.

6. C. John Miller and Barbara Miller Juliani, *Come Back, Barbara* (Phillipsburg, N.J.: P&R, 1997), 78–79.

7. Ed Welch, *Shame Interrupted* (Greensboro, N.C.: New Growth, 2012), 34.

8. Carol Barnier, *Engaging Today's Prodigal* (Chicago: Moody, 2012), 97–98.

9. D. Martyn Lloyd Jones, *Spiritual Depression* (Grand Rapids: Eerdmans, 1965), 20.

10. Philip P. Bliss, "Hallelujah, What a Savior!" (Public Domain, 1875).

11. Allender and Longman, *Bold Love*, 281.

12. Miller and Miller Juliani, *Come Back, Barbara*, 26.

13. P. T. O'Brien, *The Letter to the Hebrews* (Grand Rapids: Eerdmans, 2012), 462.

14. D. Martyn Lloyd Jones, *Romans: An Exposition of Chapters 3:30–4:25, Atonement and Justification* (Grand Rapids: Zondervan, 1970), 211.

15. John Piper, "The Sorrows of Fathers and Sons," *Desiring God*, July 15, 2009, http://www.desiringgod.org/articles/the-sorrows -of-fathers-and-sons.

16. Philip Schaff, *Eusebius Pamphilius, Church History, Life of Constantine, Oration in Praise of Constantine, NPNF2–01*, http://www .ccel.org/ccel/schaff/npnf201.iii.viii.xxiii.html.

17. Clement of Alexandria, τίς ὁ σωζόμενος πλούσιος: *Quis Dives salvetur. What Rich Man Can Be Saved?* This treatise can be found in the various editions of Clement's works.